RAMBLINGS

of an

IRISHMAN

Stories from around the world

PHILIP A. SAUNDERS

Published by

Alexander House Publications

The
UNOFFICIAL and UNABRIDGED
AUTOBIOGRAPHY

For our grandchildren - Finlay, Zoë, Miriam, Eden, and Joel
and anyone else who might be interested

I hope this fills in some of the blanks for you!

Foreword

The front cover of Philip Saunders' latest book reflects something of the quality of the contents. It invites the reader to join the writer in enjoying the view of a Madagascar seascape. But there is something more – this is a picture taken by the author through his hotel window; it is a beautiful scene shown from a unique, personal perspective, one that the reader is also invited to share.

In *Ramblings of an Irishman* Philip offers many more wonderful views – pen portraits of places he has seen and experienced in the course of a life full of travel and variety. Each chapter offers a sense of place but also a sense of the insights and experience of the writer. We learn why and how these memories are important to him. There is colour, honesty, humour, wisdom, humility, all woven together in the context of Philip's deep Christian faith and sense of God's call.

The book is a must-read companion volume to *No Ordinary Book* in which Philip tells the powerful story of his and his wife Heather's part in the team translating the New Testament into the Kouya language of the Ivory Coast, West Africa. It provides the 'before' and 'after' to that earlier account, together with many fresh insights and memories along the way.

Often when I think of the reflective work that goes into retelling a life story in paragraphs and chapters, it reminds me of building a house. So for me, it was as if with the words of *No Ordinary Book* Philip built that house, while *Ramblings of an Irishman* now provides the opportunity to accompany the owner through bright rooms, opening intriguing drawers and cupboards full of treasures and memories along the way.

In his usual unassuming manner, Philip dedicates the story to his grandchildren 'and anyone else who might be interested'. I certainly feel that this is a book which will appeal not only to those who already know Philip and something of his experiences, but also to anyone up for a delightful ramble in the company of a new friend.

Lynda Neilands

Table of Contents

Introduction

"A Path less Pursued" or "An Irishman Abroad"?

Finding an appropriate title for a book is notoriously difficult for writers. The first one above I really liked, but it sounded a bit pretentious. The second one was unfortunately already taken: far too many Irishmen want to escape the homeland, it seems.

If the title "A Road less Travelled" had been available to me, I'd have snapped it up, but Robert Frost (and Scott Peck) got there first. However, the temptation to plagiarise was immense, for it sums up beautifully what I want to write about:

The Road not Taken - By Robert Frost (1874–1963)

Two roads diverged in a yellow wood,
And sorry I could not travel both
And be one traveller, long I stood
And looked down one as far as I could
To where it bent in the undergrowth;

Then took the other, as just as fair,
And having perhaps the better claim,
Because it was grassy and wanted wear;
Though as for that the passing there
Had worn them really about the same,

And both that morning equally lay
In leaves no step had trodden black.
Oh, I kept the first for another day!
Yet knowing how way leads on to way,
I doubted if I should ever come back.

I shall be telling this with a sigh
Somewhere ages and ages hence:
Two roads diverged in a wood, and I —
I took the one less travelled by,
And that has made all the difference.

How does this apply to me? Throughout my adult life, I have always shied away from popular tourist meccas. I have been fortunate enough with my work to be able to travel to a lot of different countries, and most of them have their "must-see" sights. In my experience these often turn out to be a little disappointing, not because of the sights themselves which are often remarkable, but because of the hype and parasitic industry surrounding them. They sometimes turn out to be a way of getting you, dear visitor, into our country. Oh, and while you are here on your package tour, we will fleece you for all we are worth.

And so this has led me to look for something different

whenever I travel.

I arrive in a country for the first time. How do ordinary people live here, I ask myself? I am led to seek out the villages where there is no prepared fanfare or tidy-up for the visiting dignitary – not that I would ever fall into that category anyway – and I prefer to take public transport when it is reasonably safe to do so. I seek out the tingling experience of a chance encounter with a real wild animal on a path less pursued, rather than go on safari to gawk at animals in a zoo, even should it be a zoo without walls. One can be so intent on spotting the *Big Five* (of lion, leopard, rhinoceros, elephant, and Cape buffalo), that one misses fifty of nature's minor miracles, observable within easy reach.

In the chapters that follow then, I recount some of these travel experiences. They will take us to Madagascar, to China, and back to Ivory Coast, where my wife Heather and I spent many years working as linguists and translators. There has been great pleasure for me in meeting some fascinating people on that path, and I'd like to introduce you to them. As well as that, there are chapters from Ireland, my homeland, where we have made a foray into Ulster-Scots language and culture, travelling about in an old Bongo camper van. Lateral thinking and living intrigues both Heather and me, not just for the sake of it, but also because of what it reveals about human nature and the spice it adds to life. So, there will be a chapter about the choice we made to cramp our style, and live for a time in a glorified bed-sit.

The latter venture gave me plenty of scope to further explore the agonies and ecstasies of being married to the love of my life. The censor's pen has caused some experiences to be deleted – "You can't talk about *that*, Philip!" – but some have escaped. So you will get the idea.

And, wonder of it all, we remain married.

So much then, for the places I wanted to write about. Now for some recurring themes.

"All you are interested in is Sport and Linguistics!" exclaimed Heather.
(She did add something else, but this is a Christian book...)

You know, I can't remember the tone in which Heather originally said this: it might have been uttered with a resigned shake of the head, or in a moment of fun. For sure though, whether in jest or in judgement, there was more than an element of truth in it.

That's why you will find these themes regularly surfacing throughout all that I write here. They are known by other names, but they are indeed important to me. If truth be told, though, I have a few other passions as well. Faith in God, for instance, which permeates everything I think and do.

Belfast

'No. Stop. Put it back.'

I looked up into my mother's eyes, watched her eyebrows rise ever so slightly, and then felt her furrowed gaze bore into me. Slowly, I replaced the miniature Dinky car on top of its box on the glass display case. I stared longingly at it. I loved cars. I really loved that car. Mr. Henderson, the shopkeeper, shuffled benignly around behind his counter, oblivious to the little drama being enacted on the other side.

I was just six. Usually, I made my own way home from school, walking the mile or so by myself or with my pals, but today it was raining, so my mother had collected me. Tripping down the pavement to our home under mum's umbrella, I had fun trying to name every car that passed us by. There were few I did not know.

Next day, I was in the shop again, but this time on my own. The little car was still there, shiny and blue. Mr. Henderson turned to fetch something from the back of his shop, and I slowly lifted my hand, grasped my prize, and slipped it into the dark recesses of my school-bag. As I left the shop, my legs felt heavy, my heart was pounding, and I waited for the shout from behind me. It never came.

That evening, before tea, I played quietly by myself as usual, marshalling my cars along the ledge of the bay window. "Tea's ready, Philip!" came the call from the kitchen. "Coming, mum," I replied. "Come on now, wash your hands. We're ready," mother chided, approaching the window.

Suddenly, she stopped, and went quiet.
"Philip, is that... is that not the wee car you were looking at yesterday?"

"Where...?" I asked guiltily.

"In Henderson's shop. It is, isn't it? How did you get it?" She studied my face. "You didn't take it, did you?"

I felt my cheeks start to get hot. Mother knew the truth then.

"You're coming with me tomorrow, straight back to that shop after school, and you are going to explain yourself to Mr. Henderson. And you'll put that wee car back where it belongs! It's not yours."

And so it came about, that I had to suffer the humiliation of returning the stolen goods to their rightful owner, under the watchful eye of two adults, and of not a few of my fellow pupils on their way home from school.

It was a lesson that was to stay with me for the rest of my life.

Guiders, bows and arrows and the Black Hand Gang

Today's Health and Safety officials would have a fit. But to grow up as boys on the streets of Belfast, in a reasonably residential area, we had to create our own risky world, setting ourselves challenges outside the obvious and not always welcome academic ones set in school.

Our parents accepted that boys would be boys, and even aided and abetted us in our schemes. Our fathers helped to assemble 'guiders', a poor man's go-cart. These took all shapes and forms, but mine consisted of a wooden box to sit in, atop a frame with two wooden cross-pieces for the axles and wheels to be attached to. Smaller wheels at the front, bigger ones at the back, probably culled from dead or dying perambulators (prams). Essential was the rope attached to the front on both sides, beside the space where you could put your feet. This was for steering the guider.

Some fancy guiders had brakes of a sort, usually a piece of wood on a swivel, acting like a hand-brake. These generally got too worn out with friction on the hard pavements, so most of us didn't bother, but just wore out our shoes instead if we needed to slow down.

Slowing down was not our aim, though. We wanted to hurtle as fast as we possibly could down the steep Irwin Crescent, which was part of our home turf. This was the dangerous part, not for us, but for any unsuspecting older person struggling home with their bags of shopping, for there were blind spots. Tall and bushy privet hedges spoiled our visibility, meaning that we couldn't see pedestrians as we swung skilfully, but out of control, round the final bend into Irwin Avenue.

There were many near misses. Thus we might get a well-deserved but friendly reprimand from the Ormo bread-server, as he chugged from door to door in his purple and cream electric van.

We also had a period of intense interest in archery. I recall my pride in purchasing my first real arrow from the Athletic Stores downtown. It cost two shillings and four pence, an absolute fortune. It gave our games of Cowboys and Indians a touch of authenticity, as we let fly with our real arrows from the top of the Crescent, to see who could fire the furthest. It was like the Olympic games, without the safety measures.

Out of these escapades and camaraderie grew the Black Hand Gang. It was the only name we knew for a gang, and in retrospect, wasn't very creative. Yet the games we played were highly so, and our imaginations ran riot. We hid behind sheets of plywood, wedged upright between kerb and road, and threw real stones at each other. You know, I don't remember anyone being hurt in these street wars, which probably doesn't say much for the accuracy of our shooting!

When we tired of that, a favourite pursuit was the illicit appropriation (theft) of the ripe apples in Mrs Lightbody's back garden. That orchard ('orky') was a garden of Eden for us boys growing up, made more delicious by our illegal entry, and by an Air Raid shelter, a relic of the rather recent Second World War. And by the stolen apples of course, which meant sore tummies for all of us later on that night.

When Mrs Lightbody came out unexpectedly, we scattered, and hopped on to our tricycles. My memory is of a thinnish, white woman with grey hair shaking her fist after us, as we made off at speed down the Crescent. I discovered what adrenaline was.

Which leads me to a slightly sad emotion. About my tricycle. At an age when it was important not to be too different, my bike was red, while my fellow conspirators' bikes were both blue. They had a boot compartment at the back, I had a basket on my front handlebars. Then it seemed that their bikes went faster than mine, though admittedly that may also have had something to do with my leg muscles at the time.

Spiritual awakening

Some of the above experiences showed me, even as a young boy, that all was not well inside me. I knew right from wrong, and I knew that I was having a hard time choosing the first option.

February 14th, 1958 - St. Valentine's day - was to change my life forever. I'm not exaggerating.

My parents wanted to bring us up under the sound of the Gospel. So as if all the services and children's meetings we were expected to attend in Ballyhackamore Gospel Hall were not sufficient, on a Friday night the four of us Saunders children traipsed off to Bloomfield Baptist Church down at the Arches. Those were the days when cars were few, but you had to be wary of the electrically powered trolley buses as you crossed over the Upper Newtownards Road.

Bible truths and rousing children's choruses were the order of those evenings. But it was during a more reflective chorus that I opened up my heart to the Lord Jesus, and He came into my life to stay.

The emotion of that evening, a joy never before experienced, and the knowledge that something highly significant had changed within me, are incredibly sharp in my memory today, sixty years on.

Helen Pollock was an angel in the Strandtown Primary school play. I was a seven-year-old shepherd. She was the most beautiful creature I had known up to that point, with graceful arms gently holding up a wand to the skies. I remember very little else about her, except that she lived close to the school off Earlswood Road, wore a radiant face and a tartan skirt, and invaded my thoughts and emotions in a way a girl had not succeeded in doing up to that point in my life. She never knew the effect she had on me. After P4, I left that school for Singapore, but that angel travelled with me in my dreams, until she was eventually superseded by another heavenly creation.

P.S. A dozen years later, curiosity driving me, I went back to where I vaguely remembered her home to be, and boldly rapped on the door. What on earth was I doing?! Before I could run away, the door opened, and a kindly woman of middle age appeared. I made some stuttering comment about wondering whether this was where Helen Pollock lived? It was indeed, this was in fact her mother, but Helen was at college in England now.

What else I said I do not recall, but this was a small triumph over timidity for me. Even though it was so many years later, and even though I did not declare my undying love or anything, this nice lady was amused to realise that I had been interested in her angel of a daughter so many years before, and the whole episode was a kind of vicarious victory. Mrs Pollock no doubt gave a quiet chuckle behind her closing front door, but I left elated.

Love can make a fool of a man.

Libya

For most people I should think, memories are very hazy between the ages of two and four years. This is the period when our family was in Libya, sandwiched between that growing up experience in East Belfast.

I have only a few memories, but very vivid ones. Some of these would be influenced, no doubt, by the old photos from that time: small rectangles of black and white turning sepia, with crinkle-cut edging. Taken with Brownie cameras.

Others exist only in my mind, though. In these, the colours are stark. I see the bright orange of the citrus-fruit in our gardener Mukta's black hands, as he holds them out to us children. The sky is a hot blue. There is the dangerous black outline of the scorpion I discovered as a toddler in the garden, silhouetted on dazzling white sand. I still shiver from the fear in my mother's voice, as she pulled me back and away from my find. Then there was the white, neatly pressed shirt and shorts my father wore, and the click and tramp of his highly polished black shoes on the pathway as he left or returned from his work.

My father had been stationed in Tobruk; we lived as a family near Tripoli. I was proud of him, proud of the important job he went to each day. I knew he had met the Queen, on her visit to Libya to inspect her troops. Ghadaffi had not been heard of as yet.

And another, more troubling memory surfaces. A puzzling one. My mother had brought us children out to Libya by RAF plane, and we had overnighted in Malta in a nissen hut, she later told me. I had been excited, looking forward to seeing my father again, as he had gone on ahead of the family several months before.

But when we landed in Tripoli, he was not there to meet us. The airport was loud and noisy and filled with strange languages. Men with beards shouting and pointing. My elder brother David and I wandered off a bit, my mother stayed with our luggage. And then all of a sudden dad was there, embracing my mother, looking round at us.

He didn't recognise me at first. This is the shock, and the puzzle. I remember wondering why? He seemed just the same to me. In retrospect, it was probably because my long blond curls had now been cut off, making me look older. But soon all was ok, as he lifted me up and hugged me too.

Thirteen months we lived there: my first experience of Africa. Since my mother was an exceptional cook, and we loved giving hospitality, our house seemed always to be full of hungry, single airmen, happily luxuriating in a taste of home comforts.

Excitement, curiosity, fear, puzzlement, pride, laughter and wonder – these were some of the first sensations I experienced in life abroad. My appetite was whetted for more, no doubt about it.

Castlerock

Rock Ryan stands as a sentinel on the western end of Castlerock beach. Really "sits" or "lies" would be a more apt description, for many would think that not a lot happens in this sleepy village on the North Coast of Northern Ireland.

Rock Ryan is a handsome house of dark grey stone and white mortar, which nestles comfortably into the black rock behind it, in its turn giving shelter from the prevailing north-westerly winds that regularly sweep across the village from Donegal in winter-time.

From the building's windows you have an uninterrupted view down the beach to the Barmouth, where the River Bann flows impressively into the very extreme north of the Irish Sea. Beyond the Bann lies another stretch of strand, and then comes Portstewart, its many windows glinting and reflecting the sun setting over the Inishowen peninsula behind Rock Ryan.

In 1960, this lovely house was let out to holiday-makers over the summer, and our family stayed in it for a month. This was my introduction to Castlerock, and I marvelled at the history of the place. I pictured the monks who actually used to live in *Rock Ryan*, daily making their way down to the Monks' Pool at the Bann to get washed. Later I learned that C.S. Lewis's family spent their vacations in Castlerock, staying in a stone terrace not far from the house.

However, at eight years of age, I was not bothered about the real tangible giants of English Literature. I was more concerned with hunting out imaginary giants closer to home in the tumble of rocks behind our holiday house, beating them off and sending them back to Scotland. Just like Finn McCool had done further down the coast at the Giant's Causeway.

Of more interest to me in those warm, heady days of summer, was the freedom to roam in the sand-dunes, learning to fish in the river or the sea, or running on the beach with our dog Rover, a black and tan collie.

Grandpa Saunders came up to visit that month. We Irish love to visit each other on holidays. The familiar tempers the unfamiliar: a pleasant mix. Grandpa seemed ancient to us, but as my dad was only forty-four, *his* father can only have been about the age I am as I write – so in his prime really! Grandpa lived in Belfast with Aunty Beth, Uncle Frank, and their son Alan our cousin. He slipped us children a silver sixpence each to buy sweets, and introduced us to Fry's chocolate cream bars from the local shop, where you had to trip over buckets, spades, fishing nets and other children to gain entrance.

Yes, *Rock Ryan* watched benignly over our family's transition between Belfast and Singapore, an exotic island further away than we children could think or imagine, but about to get closer and closer as we boarded our first boat to England in August of 1960.

Taking a cruise before they were invented

It was 1960.

The slightly melancholic strains of "The Lord's my Shepherd" bounced back and forth between the walls of Belfast docks and the steel panels of our ship about to sail.

I felt embarrassed, but ashamed of myself for being so. These were our friends, come to wish us Godspeed, and see us off to foreign climes. As for me, as an eight-year-old lively boy, all I wanted was to be away, to be free to explore the boat, to race up to the bows and see where we were going next.

It was an adventure to me. And yet, looking back, I understand better. In those days of limited plane travel, when folks parted like this, they didn't know whether they would meet up again on this earth, and so the little group of friends huddled on the quayside, their waving white handkerchiefs growing smaller by the minute, was expressing that sadness in the way they knew best – by singing hymns. Nan, my mum's mother, had tearfully wondered whether she would ever see us again. It's true also that my elder brother David was remaining behind to continue his schooling at Annadale Grammar; he would be lodging with my father's cousin, Aunty Lily. So our wee family was being split up, though we knew David would come out to visit us in Singapore during his holidays.

Our final departure was from Tilbury docks in London. There, as the M.V. Benmore set sail, there was no-one singing down below. Ours was a cargo-passenger ship. Apart from the crew, there were only twelve passengers, and our family made up five of them.

I have a little silver bell, which sits on my desk. Slightly tarnished now, it reminds me of those sea journeys to and from Singapore. I smile as I pick it up by the miniature ship's wheel at the top. "P & O Cathay" it says. We came home three years later on this much larger passenger liner.

For the journey out, my younger sister Pamela and I were the only proper children on board, and we were spoiled. Hazel was almost eight years older than I was, so I classified her as a grown-up really.

The crew did their best to keep us actively involved and happy in the life of the ship. We played deck quoits, throwing circles of tough twisted rope along the varnished slippery wooden planks, trying to land them in the bullseye, or at least in one of the circles. They erected a badminton net, with other safety nets to stop the shuttlecock flying overboard. For Pamela and me, they constructed a small swimming-pool when it got hotter on the Mediterranean Sea, through the Suez Canal, and into the Red Sea. Water was poured into a waterproof canvas square, draped over a wooden framework. It was here that Pamela and I learned to swim, which stood us in good stead for the outdoor life we were going to. Some of the crew were giving other, less noble lessons too: little did I know that a Scottish seaman was teaching my younger sister how to smoke, behind the ventilation cowls. But they did let her sing

"How did Moses cross the Red Sea?" over the ship's loudspeakers as we made our way down that stretch of water!

One of the other passengers was a Mr Colin Green, a teacher taking a career break. I got to know him. He would lounge on the railing of the ship as the sun went down, stare into the distant horizon, and quietly sing "The Wild Colonial Boy". This song was wistful too, but more to my liking in this context than a hymn. We had hours to put in between ports, and Colin also taught me how to play chess, a game I grew to love. For me, the bishops, knights and pawns took on a life and personality of their own, on board the M.V. Benmore.

"Wake up, Philip!" My father was shaking my shoulder gently. "What's happening?" The ship's clanging flooded my senses. Then I remembered and was suddenly wide awake. "Are we in Aden now?" "Yes, we're there!"

I felt cold and shivered in the cool night-time air as I scrambled into some clothes.

We were all up now, and watching down below, as small vessels arrived to take us ashore. It was 3 a.m. I had never been up and outside in the middle of the night before. I was sleepy but strangely very alert. The rest of the night passed in a blur of men strangely dressed in long white robes and head-dresses, black beards and flashing eyes, taxis speeding through empty streets to shops with cameras and radios for sale. Shopkeepers sprawled across their doorways were roused from slumber. But in the morning, back on board, we admired my father's purchases, which included a radio and a pair of binoculars, so valuable for appreciating the Indian

Ocean we were about to enter.

The *Benmore* stopped at only three ports: Gibraltar, Port Said and Aden, during the three week voyage. After Aden, until we reached the Straits of Malacca between Malaya and Indonesia, we weren't to see land for a number of days. So we became accustomed to empty seas all round, with flying fish scattering to port and starboard as the *Benmore* ploughed on. To spot a tanker or another cargo-passenger boat was an event which I recorded in my notebook, watching vessels through our binoculars until they disappeared over the horizon. Long, hot, lazy days were punctuated with welcome meals, announced by Chang in his smart black and white uniform and his musical gong. Chang was the first Chinaman I had met. He left a very favourable impression, and was the first of many Chinese friends.

Singapore

If you Google "Katong" today, you will find it listed on Tripadvisor and ranked number 86 among 842 attractions in Singapore. We are advised to "Get away from the hustle and bustle and live like a local in the amazing neighbourhood of Katong."

Ah well, not everything has changed then! Sixty years ago, when our family first set foot on the island, Katong was a small village between Singapore city and my father's place of work in RAF Changi. Dad was an Electrical Engineer working for the Ministry of Public Buildings and Works, and his job was to oversee the generators which kept the RAF station operational. Similar to Armed Forces personnel and their families, his tour of duty was to last three years: 1960-1963.

We stayed for a month in the Grand Hotel, Katong, before a house nearer to Changi was identified for us. Apart from the novelty of staying in an hotel, what stands out for me were the agonisingly long siesta times. Mum and dad insisted that we stay on our beds for two whole hours after lunch each day! We didn't have to sleep, but we had to be quiet. This was no doubt wise for acclimatising to the equatorial heat and humidity, but it was also torture for my younger sister and me.

While lying on our beds, the chit-chats kept us entertained. They say that lizards are what northern foreigners first notice in tropical countries, and we kids urged them on to catch the midges and mosquitos, and smiled at the wiggling tails they jettisoned when we tried to catch the chit-chats on the walls.

Our curiosity in insect life was aroused. Ireland was so *tame* in comparison. Outside, when the temperature had finally dropped, we followed the march of the red ants along the boundary wire fence, warned by our parents not to touch them, for they would sting us. So much was new. There was so much to be explored.

After the Grand Hotel, the residence they found for us was outside Bedok, a village further along the coast towards Changi. Our home was to be in Jalan Hadji Salam. Certain memories from this location are very vivid, and indeed shaped my life's purpose in many ways.

The tarmac of Jalan Hadji Salam was hot underfoot, and burned those parts of my feet that were not protected by my worn flipflops. The sun was high, and I was making my way as quickly as I could from our house to the *kampong* at the end of our street. As I walked, the hazy mirage of greens and browns shimmering in the distance started to form itself into the more definite shapes and contours of the Malay village.

Wire mesh fences separated our house from our immediate neighbours' homes, but in contrast, the *atap* thatch village houses smiled openly at each other, and Malay folk moved around and greeted each other freely. I headed that day for the wooden veranda of a familiar house.

I had made a friend there. He was older and wiser than I, probably twenty to my nine years, and he had a typewriter while I only had a notebook. On to his machine, and into my wee book went the same words, written down in such a way that I could pronounce them properly later on, and in days to come. He taught me to count, and also the words to describe what we saw around us in that corner of the island: the sea, coconut palms, acacia and mango trees, children, men and women, the ground and the sky, the sun, moon and stars.

Back home, I would sit on top of my bed in the cool of the evening; and as the cicadas chirped outside for company and the fan pushed the air languidly around the room, I would go over the words I had learned that day, savouring their syllables, and resolving to ask my friend tomorrow for some words I could use to link them all together into sentences.

And so it was, the next day, that I learned how to say "I am going to have a swim in the sea", "I want to drink water", or "I want to eat fish", and I began to feel just a little bit more like one of those Malays I so much admired.

It was here in this *kampong* that my love of languages was born.

Yio Chu Kang

It is very difficult for a ten-year-old to get excited when he thinks nothing is happening.

And so it was for me in Yio Chu Kang assembly. When there were only a handful of believers present for gatherings, and of course only the men took part audibly apart from singing, in the open Sunday morning Breaking of Bread meeting there tended to be long moments of silence between contributions. When these did occur, there was welcome variety: a hymn or chorus, an extempore prayer, a testimony or a thought which could be from anywhere in Scripture.

In later years, I came very much to appreciate the quiet moments of meditation, but for my sister and me at that time in our lives, they were to be endured out of necessity, like siestas. Our writing skills were honed though, as we exchanged numerous notes to each other along the row of the back seat where we were required to sit, as we were not yet baptised and "in the assembly".

The local believers – many of whom were of Indian extraction - were most kind and hospitable, frequently inviting us to share exceedingly hot, spicy meals at their home!

The ever-present heat and bright sunlight beat down on the verandahs around Yio Chu Kang Gospel Hall, and crept towards us on the concrete floor, as the meetings progressed. My tendency towards claustrophobia had no chance to raise itself as a problem here, though, as the doors and shutters were all flung wide open to allow as much air and oxygen as possible to enter the building. So the daily round in this Chinese quarter of Singapore island was always highly visible through the doorways, and often proved a distraction for me in those quieter moments. I saw that Sunday was just another day for most local folk. Adjacent lay the small store, with its trickle of customers in and out, and there were the big glass jars on the wooden shelves, where Pamela and I would go afterwards to buy squares of peanut brittle with a few cents of our pocket money. Or perhaps we would choose some delicious Chinese cake made of multicoloured stripes of jelly.

While our parents and the other grown-ups continued to talk over serious matters once meeting had ended, we would clamber down the slope into the wide monsoon drains, and help local kids catch the tiny fish, the guppies. We took our turn to pull the string, attached to the neck of a jam jar, upstream against the flow of water from the culverts. The male guppies, with their rainbow colouring, were surprisingly slim and lively; by contrast, the females were plain and often heavily pregnant, no doubt carrying around with them the cares of the world. Often the reward for our endeavours was a jam jar full of little fish, male and female, which we transferred to a larger receptacle at home, and for several days we would be carefully inspecting the tank for the advent of more little ones.

There were no Health and Safety officers present to disapprove and warn us against possibly contracting noxious diseases in the monsoon drains, but somehow we survived against the odds.

Bras Basah Road assembly, which we attended upon arrival in Singapore for the first year, was a different kettle of fish.

It was a sizeable assembly with plenty going on. We went to English service, but there were meetings conducted in Chinese dialects too. The congregation was large and multicultural, and we made several lifelong friends. There were excellent Bible teachers, but one could not always control interventions in an open meeting, and it was here that I heard an elder have to ask a person to be seated, cutting him short in the middle of his homily – a very rare event. Usually, there was a flow of connected and appropriate thoughts in open assembly meetings, inspired by the Spirit in a marvellous way.

Every Sunday, after evening service, we looked forward to refreshments around long tables in the open garden behind the assembly building. This was a chance to socialise, and get to know many interesting people. I was able to pursue my fascination for language learning. One who helped me was called Soon Shi. I thought this was hilarious, and asked him was he thinking of being a girl any time soon? He indulged me my childish joke, and taught me the difference between *kelapa* and *kepala* in Malay. One was a 'coconut' and the other the word for 'head'.

"Very important to distinguish!" he exclaimed, and he was right. I took a mental note of this (in my *kepala*).

Changi

"Run, the fire-jeep's coming!"

My pals and I were not allowed to be there. But the old, burnt out Dakota was an ideal place to play, and accessible to us from the RAF station. Down through the long parched grass, across the wide monsoon drain, a few more yards and we were there. We hoisted each other up and onto the ancient plane, used for fire practice on the airfield at RAF Changi.

There was an attraction about the old Dakota. The perspex windows, that particular smell of old canvas seats and straps, caked with dust now. The disused instruments and panel of dials. Hearts in mouths as we inched our way out and along the hot, silvery wings, with the ground dangerously far below us. All this was mesmerising for us boys growing up. Some intrepid sisters were permitted to accompany us.

But we weren't supposed to be there. Planes – mostly Hastings – were landing and taking off not so far away. Then every so often, we'd spot the red land-rover kicking up clouds of dust behind it, heading straight towards us! Excitement! Off the plane we would scramble, falling over each other in our haste to cross the monsoon drain, and back to the safety of the long grass. There we crouched down, hearts thumping.

No doubt, the firefighters in the jeep had a quiet chuckle to themselves, as they headed back towards the control tower. Those were the days, it seemed, when we had a lot of freedom to play, and barbed wire fences were few and far between.

We kids all had to attend school in Changi, of course, but only from first thing in the morning, until noon. After lunch, we were free again, and for the hottest part of the day our mothers understandably took the line of least resistance, and headed for the swimming-pools, either at the Officers' Club, or the Soldiers and Airmen's Club. There our mothers sat in the shade, chatting slowly in the heat, while we children raced in and out of the pool, stopping perhaps for an icy Coke, Pepsi or Miranda. In those days, it mattered whether you were a Coke kid, or a Pepsi person. As the sun started to sink in the West, when adults became more conscious and active, and my dad arrived from his work nearby, he would take me down to the rocks and watch me fish in the sea. I marvelled at the colour and variety of the fish we could catch there, with tiny hooks baited with a sliver of prawn. Some of them I would recognise from my pictorial stamp collection; now and again even now, I take these stamps out and admire them to this day. A little piece of Singapore has followed me around the world.

Those were the days of competition. Swimming galas, when I won medals for breast-stroke, but wondered why I couldn't excel at crawl. Football tournaments, where we played as RAF Changi Primary against the Army schools and the Naval Base team. I gravitated naturally towards goals, and goal-keeper became my position for life, it seemed. First for my primary school, and more than twenty years later, for the Dema village team in Ivory Coast. In between times, I couldn't escape the nets either, playing hockey for secondary school and university, and then in the Northern Irish leagues.

Oddly enough, both my father, my two sisters and my brother all played goal-keeper too. What did that say about us as a family? Were we mere spectators in life? Were we ultra defensive? I preferred rather to believe that we were all endowed with a special sense of responsibility, and didn't mind carrying the can for others' mistakes. But then, you can put a spin on anything!

In class in the mornings, we young students accumulated knowledge in a calm environment conducive to learning. Secretly, we boys admired the pretty girls in our class, and no doubt there was something reciprocal going on too. But at that age, it was mostly relationship at a distance, as it was more important to gain street credit by bonding with your own sex for now.

I dug out my old reports from RAF Changi primary school: they were fun to read. Mr Booton, my teacher for the last two years of Primary School, probably got it about right when he commented: *Has leadership abilities, but needs to control his sense of humour at times*. So I have been trying to do so ever since. You can't imagine all that humour screaming to get out! However, he did choose me to be the judge in our regular mock court sessions, and I felt important sitting up high at the front. Come to think of it, though, it was probably Mr Booton's way of checking that sense of humour: judges have to keep an impartial poker face, after all! From a joker to a poker.

But really, for us boys of eleven years, what happened outside of class was more significant. Coming up to midday, the gharries – single-decker coaches painted air-force blue with the red, white and blue circular insignia prominent – began to assemble in the playground, ready to transport us safely home to all parts of eastern Singapore, but mostly within the boundaries of the extensive RAF station. Now each gharry had a number, and some were new, square, flash and fast, while others were old, curved and battered, but had skilful Indian drivers. It mattered a lot to us boys whether old gharry 13 managed to overtake flash gharry 18 on the journey home. So the excitement as we passed and gave its occupants the thumbs-down I remember well. I also recall the disapproval of the upper school prefects, whose job it was to control us. All part of the fun.

RAF base life was more sheltered, but the early days of living in Katong and Bedok had given me a distinct taste for real local life, rather than the artificial expatriate life in Changi, enjoyable though it was too. So I relished visits to nearby Changi village, with its Chinese restaurants and cooking stalls, the perfumed alleys of the Indian clothing merchants, the calm workshops of Malay artisans. A regular treat for Pamela and myself was to buy an ice-ball – ground up ice injected with pink or brown flavouring, which you sucked until the colour all finally disappeared. Then you threw it at your sister.

Up until that point in my life, I had had little contact with anything other than Brethren assemblies or Baptist churches. That was all I knew, and in Singapore this influence continued, as our family worshipped first in the large Bras Basah Road assembly, and later in the small Yio Chu Kang assembly. But in Changi Primary we had daily school assemblies conducted in the Church of England tradition, with occasional sorties to a C of E church on base. The songs we sang there had a singular appeal through the beauty of their melody and poetry. And they stuck in the mind of this impressionable young boy:

"Hobgoblin, nor foul fiend
Can daunt his spirit;
He knows he at the end
Shall life inherit…"

I savoured the words.

"…Then fancies fly away
I'll fear not what men say;
I'll labour night and day
To be a pilgrim."

Nor was it only a case of proclaiming truth and applying it personally. I regularly joined in earnest intercession "for those in peril on the Sea", beseeching God to

"bless those fishermen,
 and bring them back to me."

I was growing in my spiritual understanding. It struck me not simply that there were different ways to worship the God I loved, but also that I was just a small part of a great and long line of believers, whose vocabulary and command of the English language I could only marvel at.

Thaipusam, a Hindu festival

It was downtown Singapore, and our family had joined the throngs in the streets to witness the annual Thaipusam festival.

The Indian women had come out in force. Gorgeous turquoise and saffron saris, red dots on foreheads, flashing eyes and white smiles. But the noise! And the thick smoke of rising incense. I heard frantic drumming as I peered around and between the adults to try to get a glimpse of what was going on.

What I saw made me shudder. Men in a trance. Men in pain, devotees lurching along with heavy wooden *Kavadis* on their shoulders, tiny pots of goat's milk swinging from hooks on their back. Across the roadway were other congregations of brown bodies covered in white powder, busy putting sharp skewers through dark cheeks and tongues. And strangely, no blood that I could see. Weird. Frightening to me as a boy. Adults cheering and clapping the violence. And then with a crescendo of drumming, everyone's head turned, and I watched as a whirling dervish approached. His body was covered with what looked like a bird cage, points of long skewers pierced his torso everywhere; he clutched them as he danced down the narrow aisles of the clapping crowds.

I witnessed other things that day that have refused to quit my imagination over the years. Men in loin cloths running over hot coals, their feet sizzling. And yet people smiling, taking photographs...

I stuck close to my mother in the white heat of that day. "Why are they doing this?" I asked her. "They are trying to please their gods. It's their penance," she answered. I bit my lip. All these poor people, suffering all this pain, to please their gods.

Why would their gods demand such penance and torture? "My yoke is easy, and my burden is light" Jesus had said. But this all seemed so hard. Why were they beating themselves up?

I knew for sure that this was not worshipping the God whom I had come to know and love. Something was very wrong. That much was clear to me even as a boy.

I had had enough. Turning back to find our parked car, I had no wish to go back and witness any more.

However, we had other family outings which were more positive.

The Botanical Gardens with its exotic plants and cheeky monkeys which stole our peanut pokes; Labrador Point nature reserve with its relics of World War 2; the Tigerbalm Gardens; the grand Raffles hotel named after Sir Stamford Raffles, the founder of "modern Singapore", who turned it into a free port two hundred years ago. Then there was Orchard Road with its air-conditioned department stores, including the renowned C K Tang's: we still own an intricate china tea-set given to us as a Christmas present by the shop management.

For me, though, it was the trips by small boat to the outlying islands which stood out. Pulau Ubin, to the East off Singapore, was our favourite. Small wooden boats would ferry us out from Singapore harbour or Changi Point, across the calm green sea, and leave us as willing castaways for a day on small unspoilt islands, where we snorkelled, barbecued, ate pineapples, grew increasingly lobster red, and had lots of fun on the palm-fringed beach. There, in the calm bays and round the coral reefs, we marvelled at the variety and colour of tiny exotic fish which since that time we have only ever seen on postage stamps or in the confines of a household aquarium.

I can hardly call it a war wound, as there was very little unpleasant about those halcyon days, but I do have a scar on my right elbow which reminds me of one island trip. As we approached the barnacled pier after a long day out in the sun, I carelessly left the said elbow over the side of the boat as we landed. It got jammed and the blood flowed. Yet one such small incident could not detract from the absolute pleasure of boat trips to islands like Pulau Ubin.

Much of the joy of those days out was the sense of escape they afforded. Escape from the everyday round of work and school, yes, but also escape from the intense humidity. Bathing and swimming lifted the morale enormously, but so also did vacations on higher ground.

Fraser's Hill and Cameron Highlands were the preferred destinations. These uplands were some distance away, in the central plateau of the Malay peninsula. To reach them, we had to cross the Causeway to Johore Bahru on the mainland, then up further north via Malacca, where we often stopped off with Irish missionary friends, the Bentleys.

At last, though, our maroon and grey Vauxhall Cresta would

be following our friends' Volkswagen Beetle up Fraser's Hill towards our holiday in a cool climate. The road was tortuous, but we kids felt no fear as we peered down over the fern-clad slopes, only excitement. It was doubtless a fearsome trip for our mother, even though dad was an accomplished driver: she had a vivid imagination, and was of nervous disposition at such times.

We went in a group of several families along with single folk we had got to know well. Those were days of family fun, of board games, tennis matches, of adults disengaged from work and entering into our lives as children. My future brother-in-law David Hare was a keen naturalist, whose knowledge of plants, flowers, fish, birds or butterflies constantly astounded me; he and I would go hunting in the surrounding forest with our butterfly nets, and he taught me how to kill them quickly and humanely in a jar, and then mount them to show them off in all their glory. Emerald high-flyers, sword-tails, swallow-tails, death's head hawk-moths – it was a whole new, fascinating world for a ten year old boy.

The Fish Ponds

Certainly, I was captivated by the thrill of the hunt at that age, typified by chasing butterflies, spotting new birds, and catching fish.

The fish ponds presented a different challenge from fishing in the sea. There was an element of artificiality in it, to be sure, but what it lost in naturalness, it gained in excitement.

These very large ponds were stocked with several kinds of fish, and you paid per day to try to catch them. The water was murky, so even the most amateurish fisherman would not easily disturb his prey.

There were carp out there in the middle of the pond, very large specimens too, but harder to catch than the active tilapia nearer to shore. Some fishermen cast their lines out a long way, baited with round balls of tapioca infused with scented spices, and patiently sought shade under the nearby clumps of bamboo while they waited for their big moment. My pals and I, however, used worms as bait, and our hearts raced as we followed our bobbing floats' progress over the calm surface. We were continually striking, it seemed, as the greedy tilapia gobbled up our offerings. With large mouths, they were not difficult to hook. In this way we learned a lot about the art of fishing – baiting, waiting for the best moment, unhooking without damaging, releasing the fish to fight another day.

A day at the fish-pond was absorbing, and great fun. It increased our confidence and competence as fishermen, and it gave us some foundation for future, trickier battles with shy, intelligent fish inhabiting clearer streams and lakes - creatures which were pickier about what they ate, and whose meal-times were not so predictable.

Durian

"Uncle Jim" Allen drove rapidly through the deserted streets of Kuala Lumpur, while I lay moaning across the back seat of his silver-grey Riley Pathfinder.

Dad and Jim talked in low, serious voices in the front. The neon lights of city buildings flew past my window.

All I knew was that it was the middle of the night, and I had awakened with a sharp pain in my stomach. We were on our way to the hospital.

The rest of the journey and the rest of the night passed in a blur. I just remember the relief when the pain finally subsided. They kept me in the hospital for another night, and it was strange for me to be sleeping in a place where I knew nobody. Only once had I been in hospital before – to get my tonsils out – and all I recall from that was the dried blood on my pillow in the morning, and the liberal helpings of ice-cream they served me.

They figured it had been the durian fruit I had eaten the day before. On the way up the Malay peninsula from Singapore, we would break the long journey to Kuala Lumpur by calling at friends' houses, and this time we had stopped off at a village near Klang, where a lady missionary called Daphne King served the local community. Kind and hospitable, she had also served us up with segments of durian, a very strong smelling local fruit. I enjoyed it at the time, but obviously, I had not had the stomach for it. I would have to stick to pineapples, mangos and bananas – no hardship there, with such delicious alternatives!

Life sometimes threw up the unexpected, I realised. Life was precarious. Life was precious, and to be treasured.

Despite the odd mishap, we children always looked forward to these road trips. The route linking Singapore island with Malaya's capital, Kuala Lumpur, was 250 miles long, sometimes along the coast, sometimes through the extensive rubber plantations with mile after mile of little cups catching the precious white latex leaking from the tree trunks.

When we finally stopped at the Bentleys' house, or the Allens' bungalow, the grown-ups started their catch up session over tea, while we had hours of fun to look forward to with the children of these families. Tom Bentley was a well-known Bible teacher in Malacca, while Jim Allen was administrator of a Teacher Training college in "K. L." The common denominator was that we were all Irish, and the Irish abroad enjoy getting together! These friendships stood the test of time. But next day, or the day after that, it was off again for the next leg of our holiday, perhaps to Fraser's Hill as previously mentioned, or to cross by car-ferry to the island of Penang, with its brilliantly white strands and its funicular railway.

Stopping off or visiting missionaries gave me insights into the marvellous work they were engaged in, but while I had great admiration for them, I never saw myself doing what they did. It was only when I heard about Bible translation work at seventeen years of age, that something inside me clicked in response. This could be what I am supposed to do in life, I thought.

Castlerock 2

At eleven years of age, my family and I returned to Ireland after three years in Singapore. We rented a terrace house in Castlerock, not too far from RAF Ballykelly, where dad was now stationed for a year.

It was September, grey and rainy. Sighs and umbrellas. The green double-decker bus bounced and splashed the six miles from Castlerock to Coleraine, where it discharged its reluctant students, headed for the town's grammar schools.

I felt over-dressed and awkward in my heavy jacket and long grey trousers. Classrooms were pokey and airless, windows too high to look through or escape from. Teachers seemed mostly tyrannical to a sensitive first-former, and fights broke out every break-time, ignored by the staff, flocked to by pupils.

An alien in an alien land is how I felt. Deprived of sun and oxygen, I was in danger of dying a slow death.

But the most popular boy in my class liked me. He called me

Sambo, due no doubt to my deep Singapore tan. At lunchtime, space was created in the crowded playground for football with a tennis ball. New jackets were thrown down for goals, pristine shoes became old before their time.

But I loved this break from the drudgery of class, and what seemed like the aimlessness of the usual pupil interactions.

Here in the playground, for a time, there was passion, purpose, rules I could understand or get to know quickly, a chance to succeed and know it, a way to become accepted. Sport became for me the great leveller, where we all played by the same rules, and skill was recognised.

Gradually Sambo became, no longer an oddity, but someone who was tolerated and even liked. And the other boys did not seem to resent it when I did well in classwork either.

Caddying

It was during this year in Castlerock that I discovered the joys of being alone. New relationships in school were an effort, but I could regain peace and equilibrium when by myself.

Our family was welcomed into the small Brethren assembly in Brook Street, Coleraine, and my Sunday school teacher was a very kindly man, though my prize of *The Sermons of George Whitefield* was a little advanced for my understanding. I still preferred Biggles and Gimlet at that age.

So I loved to escape school and relational complications and head for the sand-dunes, where I would wander and explore for hours, with the surf beating comfortingly in the distance, and the wind refreshing my senses.

Throughout that winter of 1963 I learned to become a caddy. 'My man', a Dr Watson who had retired to the seaside village, paid me six shillings and six pence to pull his cart round the eighteen holes, no matter what the weather. My young eyes were sharp, and able to follow the line of his golf balls, so as a combination we were successful. Through my first regular employment, then, I learned that work can be fun, enjoyable and lucrative, if you find the working environment in which you can thrive.

Other caddies were paid seven bob, but 'their men' did not come every week, and they would be left listless and abandoned outside the clubhouse. At least my man, though not the best golfer, and certainly not the snazziest dresser, turned out to be Mr Reliable, always arriving for his round in waterproofs and horn-rimmed glasses.

So three or four hours later I would go home to get warmed up with a mug of hot chocolate, and with several silver coins jingling in my pocket.

Holywood

Who would pick up and read a biography entitled "My Happy Life"?

No-one, I'm guessing. Real life is not one endless sequence of happy days; light and shade are part of its intrinsic interest.

So it is at the risk of losing my reader, that I declare the four years in Holywood, Co Down, to be among the happiest of my life.

During these years I was able to pursue the significant aspirations I mention elsewhere: unlimited sports, my first real girlfriend, and study of languages at secondary school.

That school was Sullivan Upper. Rory McIlroy the golfer was *another* famous alumnus... Yes, and in Latin classes, we learned to decline words like *alumnus-i masculine* - I grew to enjoy that language increasingly for its structure, and its insights into an ancient civilisation.

Then this was the first mixed secondary school I had attended:

the classroom ethos was one of mutual respect between boys and girls, and the teachers clearly enjoyed their work and appreciated their colleagues. Having a comparatively small number of boys to choose from compared to the big Belfast schools, Sullivan rarely made the grand finals. Yet the school punched above its weight in rugby, hockey and cricket, and the teams were renowned as some of the best losers in the Province! Which was very nice and all, but it was scant compensation for some of us more competitive youngsters.

Pupils had nicknames for teachers. In the current era of exaggerated political correctness, we would probably be pilloried for uttering them, for some reason or another. But here are some of the more harmless ones. "Wee Pug" taught me Latin; "The Rab" taught me Geography; "Tommy"(Hooks) taught history; I had "The Bun" for French and German, my favourite subjects along with Latin; Fanny Erskine was the Art teacher, and Big Stanley "Jasper" Mills taught English and was a legend in Scripture Union circles. Last but definitely not least, "Freezer" alias Jack Frost was a headmaster who ruled with a rod of iron (figuratively speaking), and thus made the disciplinary side of the teacher's job that much easier. Teacher and student alike relaxed, so there was much harmless fun and banter in the corridors of Sullivan Upper school.

We lived in the village of Holywood: from my bedroom, I had a view over the Belfast Lough to Jordanstown and Carrickfergus castle. The short walk to school took me less than ten minutes. I often day-dreamed during the structured daily lessons, but looked forward to extra-curricular pursuits. Friendships were formed during shove ha'penny on the teacher's table at break; long, serious chess matches developed focus and concentration. After school, if there were no organised sports, we honed our cricketing skills in the nets, or released pent-up energy in the table-tennis club. There was something for everyone, new aspirations and ambitions, where an early teenage boy could forget his growing pains, and tumble, exhausted, into bed as another day drew to a close.

But then, all of a sudden... life became more complicated.

I was fourteen, going on fifteen.

My whole family went on holiday to Greystones in the South of Ireland, joining with other families at *Carrig Eden*, a large Christian holiday home beside the sea. Parents, sons and daughters, we all lived together for family week in this mansion, tiring ourselves out happily by swimming, competing in games, climbing hills and not sleeping enough.

This was the week that I realised that I liked girls. In particular, I really loved that particular girl. There were moonlit walks in a boisterous group. She was part of it. There were outings to the fish and chip shop, all piled into cars driven by seventeen-year-olds. She was beside me in the back of the car. For the first time ever, I felt the electric tingle of attraction. I had eyes for her alone.

The course of true love was not smooth. The angel I admired, even at that tender age, belonged to another. Yes, a precocious young man - too handsome by far in my opinion -

had won the maiden's heart during the previous week, before my family arrived at camp.

Yet she was so close. As I reached out in my mind to take her hand, a voice from within whispered:

"No, Philip. She doesn't belong to you. Hands off!"
Reluctantly, I complied.

A week or so later, after my family had returned home, a letter dropped through our door. It was addressed to me! There was my name and address, carefully composed in turquoise fountain-pen. I retired to my room to open it carefully, away from my prying sister's curiosity.

It was from my angel. The one I had loved from afar, the one I had chivalrously allowed my rival to possess. I had stepped back for the whole family holiday week. And now my restraint was vindicated. It turned out that she was now free, and wanted to return my affections.

Reader, you'll not believe it, but ten years later, I ended up marrying her. Not before experiencing a rollercoaster of emotions, from the dread of having lost her to someone else, to the giddy heights of finally getting engaged.

But more of that later.

In January 2019, fifty years after living there, I used my travel pass and took the train back to Holywood. Just for a wee dander down memory lane.

Walking up through the small town, every other establishment seemed to be either an attractive little café, or a rather up-market charity shop. There was a sprinkling of glass-fronted hairdressing salons, a few churches, a bookie's, and the pavement population was a mixture of smart young professionals, and elderly retired folk. As I ambled along, I dodged the rollators in front of me, while being overtaken by the young set in the fast lane. There was an air of courteous affluence, with "lunch" and "golf" the most frequently recorded words.

This was not how I remembered High Street, Holywood. Clearly, the four-lane bypass had made a difference. But while there might have been a danger of the village becoming a backwater, there was still enough going on socially to make the place lively.

I approached the gates of Sullivan Upper, my old school, and was pleased to see the hockey and rugby pitches in great condition beside the curve of the driveway. The old pavilion had been tastefully replaced, solar panels were discreetly hidden on the back roof of the main building to collect whatever sun power they could from behind the Holywood hills. In fifty years it had not changed too much, with minor, subtle improvements in appearance. More than I could say about myself, I lamented.

Now I was on the Belfast Road, which had formerly connected Belfast with Bangor as the main arterial highway. I wandered slowly past no. 30, where we had lived. The whole row of fine houses had stood the test of time well. Our lawn had been narrowed to create more driveway and car space, but youngsters would still be able to play cricket there as we had - scoring a 2 into the hedge along the ground, a 4 into the hedge without bouncing, and a 6 and out anywhere outside the garden perimeter.

There was now a new Baptist church down the hill, beside a Spar supermarket and petrol station – this made me wonder whether we could or should actually move back here for our final hurrah on earth? But no, the friends we enjoyed then were long gone from Holywood or had moved house, and to live there we would daily run the risk of sinking back too soon into the comfortable sofa of our memories.

I turned left, towards the hills. Climbing up the long, steep rise of Jackson's road I felt my legs ache, which youthful ones had never seemed to do. On my right, behind two barriers of a tall fence and a wall, were the dark brown dwellings for Palace Barracks' residents. My father had walked to work here, back in the day.

Turning left to continue the circular tour, I passed Redburn estate on my right, and the White City estate on my left. Along Demesne Road, past the Holywood Golf club where – in no particular order of importance - I honed my caddying skills, and Rory McIlroy developed his driving prowess. Down through the White City again, where private ownership and newbuilds had transformed what was always an attractive estate. Sneaking then through the side entrance of Sullivan, and down the main driveway, I figured that even not-so-famous alumni would not be challenged for trespassing. Banners with team pictures proclaimed victory in finals for the school's hockey and rugby players, which gave me a certain glow of satisfaction somehow. Perhaps now at last, we were known as "good winners" as well as "good losers"!

From there, it was back down along the pavement which I used several times on a Sunday, when I walked with my siblings to the Gospel Hall off High Street. The old Hall was now an accountancy office it seemed, but a new one had been built close by. Across the road from the two halls was a tanning studio, not there before, but perhaps necessary because of the rarity of strong sun in Holywood, County Down. The village's name was pronounced "Hollywood", just as in that place of actors' dreams far away, but there the similarity between the two places probably ended.

However, as I made my way back down contentedly to catch the train back home, I knew for sure that day which location I would prefer to live in.

Hereford

Burghill

My father, Eric Saunders, liked living in England. He was pleased to get a posting to Credenhill, to live in Herefordshire. To my sister Pamela and myself, now in mid-teens, it was clear he got a new lease of life once he set foot on English soil, away from the constraints of N Ireland.

Burghill village church was his choice of Brethren assembly for us to attend as a family. He could have picked Barton Road hall in Hereford city instead, where he had once heard the great Dr Martyn Lloyd-Jones preach in his youth - this was a larger company of believers. However, dad preferred to be a big fish in a small pond rather than the reverse: he liked to feel he was making a worthwhile contribution to the life of the church. And his undoubted leadership qualities shone through in this more restricted environment.

So it was there that we worshipped for two years, my A level years, in a small country gathering of perhaps two dozen folk, wending our way to the tiny chapel three times of a Sunday:

morning meeting, Sunday school, and evening Gospel service – following the familiar pattern in most places we had been to all over the world.

On Sunday morning, the Breaking of Bread meeting, only the men would take part of course, which meant there was just a handful of potential contributors. This meant in turn that the men would pray and teach at length, in order to fill the allotted time. There were often long periods of silent prayer and devotion too, and personally I grew to love those times of reflection without embarrassment that no-one was talking. We were "waiting on the Spirit and each other", though the pauses did nothing to discourage my innate propensity to daydream.

As in a regular small family, one got to know the characters in the church, and who did what when. There was much predictability. Predictability in how Gwyneth the organist slowly turned over the pages of her hymnbook, and shuffled in her seat before hitting the first note; in how Glyn her husband made sure the seats were arranged in orderly, reverent fashion before the service; without fail, there would be a pristine white cloth spread on the central table around which we sat, with the loaf of bread and cup of wine carefully positioned on it. Then young but tall Philip Randall would pick up and store the hymnbooks after morning service, and saintly old Mr Fowler would praise the Lord at length in his rich Herefordshire accent, winding down to close his prayer like an aeroplane threatening to land several times before actually touching down safely.

My dad took the Bible class of a handful of young people,

including my sister Pamela and myself, and Sunday evening meeting was led by visiting speakers, who did not raise their voices to harangue us as many Irish preachers did, but reasoned persuasively from the Scriptures. This appealed to me more: I found I could actually hear what they were saying directly, without having to keep a surreptitious finger in one ear to cut down the noise from the platform.

The Burghill believers were welcoming and lovely. Yet overall, to lively teenagers, such a small gathering risked being as stifling as the hot and sultry hedgerows and agricultural land surrounding it, where the pollen hung heavy, and made many of us sniffle from summer colds, as well as the customary winter ones.

Depression

It was during these two years in Hereford that I first experienced depression in a deeper way.

It was almost inevitable, given the sense of bereavement upon leaving behind strong friendships in Ireland. Heather and I had continued to write to each other on all sorts of issues, meeting up now and again as family programmes allowed. I was also missing a happy school life in Holywood.

In comparison, Hereford High School for boys seemed soul-less. There was very little Christian influence, fellow-pupils seemed to have reached sixth form with feelings of disenchantment, cynicism and a desire to leave school as soon as possible. The buildings in downtown Hereford seemed cramped and functional.

Languages were not the school's strong point either. For my A levels, there were three in French class, two in Latin, and one in German. My German teacher, who came out of retirement to teach me, was superb – exacting and not accepting my at times hazy understanding of German lexical roots and structures. My French teacher was extremely pleasant, my Latin master very much old-school and proclamatory, rather than interactive, even though the class was tiny.

At the same time I was trying to establish an identity separate from my parents: I was in the process of leaving adolescence. This was painful for my father and me especially, as I could never be a "chip off the old block" as he might have wished. I had countless theological and ecclesiastical questions, so I tended to bounce these off Heather, to whom I continued to write long letters.

Painful Incidents stand out in my memory. I thrived when playing sport, so on a Saturday morning I might be playing rugby for the school, hockey in goals for Hereford City in the afternoon, and table-tennis in the evening! On one occasion, after a hockey match, I was in the lounge with the other guys having a drink (orange juice for me), when my dad entered, obviously angry, and got me to leave with him.

It turned out that he felt I should have been at home by now, and what was I doing fraternising with drinkers in a bar? For me at that time, and probably still, it was not the external influences which contaminated, though one had to be generally careful of the company one kept; rather it was the attitude and engagement or otherwise of your heart which mattered. 'If you kept yourself totally apart from others, how could you have any effect on them?' I reasoned in my adolescent way.

The episode brought into sharp relief different interpretations of what it meant to be 'in the world, but not of it.' At the time, my father and I had differing perspectives on separateness. But then, I had grown up in a sheltered Christian family, while he had rubbed shoulders with the roughest elements the world had to offer, and he doubtless feared my keeping bad company.

And so, I felt I was trapped in a system I didn't believe in one hundred per cent. I felt hemmed in, and so escaped to an inner world which was not a healthy solution. Anger turned inward causes depression, I later discovered, but at that age I couldn't analyse it, I just felt it.

As teenagers, then, both my sister Pamela and I were glad when the time came to return to Belfast to our friendship circles, and where many companies of believers were larger. We felt able to breathe again, and soak in the life and variety on offer there.

First taste of Switzerland

And yet, even though there were times when I felt down and depressed in Hereford, missing the intimacy of Sullivan Upper School and closer proximity of Heather, there were some bright spots to keep up my morale.

I passed my driving test; I earned some pocket-money by working for Findus Frozen Foods and in a strawberry canning factory. Playing senior hockey meant I visited many beautiful parts of South Wales, Herefordshire, Gloucestershire and Worcestershire.

Then between Lower and Upper Sixth forms, I made my first solo flight. I mean, there were other folk in the plane, but nobody else I knew. I flew to Kloten airport outside Zurich, where I was collected by old friends Hans and Gertrud Brunner-Keller, who had also been on holiday in *Carrig Eden*, Greystones, the year Heather and I met. They had offered the chance to visit their country, to help me improve my German. They promised they would speak High German to me, but I greatly anticipated hearing more Swiss German spoken too, which some maintain is the language of heaven!

Frau Brunner often seemed amused at the antics of this young Irishman, but enjoyed my attempts at their heavenly tongue. "Ach, du meine Güte!" – "Good gracious me!" she would exclaim, laughing.

Pushing back the wooden shutters, and leaning out of the window of my room that first still, sultry evening in the village of Wettingen, I admired the neighbouring, brown and white chalet-style houses with their window boxes of geraniums. The fragrance of apricots drifted up from the garden below. Everything was so sharp, so clean and cared for. "Yes, I like this place," I thought.

The Brunners had arranged for me to spend a week working for the CVJM (YMCA), who were building a centre on the

Hasliberg, a mountain in the Bernese Uplands. A crowd of youthful volunteers from all over Europe were to join in the effort. My job that week turned out to be digging trenches, the foundations for a new community chalet. It was an absolute pleasure. Every five minutes I would look up from my work, and my gaze would drift up the lush green lower slopes, to the foothills, to the outline of the distant snow-covered Matterhorn, set in its sky-blue frame.

In the evenings, we young ones learned to sing and dance to folk-songs and choruses in the different languages represented: Czech, French, Israeli and of course, Swiss. This burned off any residual energy we might have had. We sang the Hokey Pokey in Swiss German. As it happened, on the very last night I got chatting to a Swiss girl who was a particularly good listener... This was very good for my German. Her name was Sylvia Zollinger.

After returning to Wettingen, I decided I needed more personal German tuition, so to Frau Brunner's amusement, I enquired about trains into Zurich. All I knew was that Sylvia was an Art Student at college in the city. Helpfully, Frau Brunner explained where the main college was, though warned me that there were several subsidiary ones. The twinkle in her eye told me she thought I wasn't half wise.

Undeterred, I set off on my little adventure, to find an attractive needle in a Swiss haystack.

You'll have learned from much of my history that love always seems to find a way, and so it was in this case too. I watched as crowds of students streamed out of classes from the main

Art College, and lo and behold, there was the lady in question! As she came out into the sunlight, she was chatting animatedly to a friend, unmistakeable with that bouncy gait of hers I had admired so much in the Bernese mountains.

"Ach, du meine Güte!" (That phrase again) "Du bist's, Philip? Was machst du denn hier?"

The chatty girlfriend kind of melted away, and the two of us took off for an exquisite afternoon walking endlessly round the cobbled streets of old Zurich. How my German seemed to improve by leaps and bounds that day.

I did catch my train back to Wettingen though, which left on time. Swiss trains *always* run on time! So do Swiss cooks. Frau Brunner had an apricot flan just out of the oven when I rounded the kitchen door, exactly what this ravenous German student needed.

Dublin

1970 was a great year to be alive and nineteen, and first term at Trinity College, Dublin was an exciting time to start student life. Inevitably, there was some apprehension too. There would be a leap in expectation academically: would I be able to make it, or would I fall short? I had succeeded in my own little spheres at the schools I'd attended, but this was different. All my contemporaries had attained high grades, many of us had enjoyed excellent coaches on the way through, but now the boat had been pushed out on the unpredictable waves of academia.

Students reacted to the new challenge in a variety of ways. Most attended lectures, but in between, the need for social popularity or escapist entertainment took over. Until, that is, an assignment had to be submitted, when panic and caffeine saw them through.

For myself, I led a rather limited life, partly on purpose, partly by default. I stuck to the comfort zones of study, which I enjoyed, and of sport, playing hockey on the university's teams. I joined in where possible with the Christian Union's activities, pursuing deeper relationships with a natural network of friends, old and new.

During first term, I was a boarder with Mrs Warwick, a genteel older lady living alone in an old three storey terrace house in Baggott Street, about half an hour's walk from the university. For seven guineas a week, she provided half board, and joined me for evening meal and tea from china cups I was afraid I would drop.

This pleasant win-win situation was not to last, however.

Loud hammering on my bedroom door in the middle of the night ripped me from a peaceful slumber. Muffled shouts had me instantly wide awake. I moved across to the door, and opened it. "Get out, get out!" yelled someone. Looking downstairs, I saw the wooden bannisters silhouetted against smoke and licking flames. I ran back to my bedroom window and looked down. No way of escape there! Back to the inner door, grabbing my coat from a chair on the way.

Next I knew, I was out on the pavement, cold under my bare

feet, looking back at the smoke billowing out of the main door and upstairs windows. Mrs Warwick was out already, a person supporting each of her arms. The other lodger from the top floor, whom I didn't really know, ran to and fro in agitation. He must have been the one who had wakened me. I looked at my watch: 3 a.m.

The rest of the night is a blur in my memory. Fire-engine arriving, hoses deployed, steam, black smoke, and shivering with cold and adrenaline. Then being bundled into a car, and taken off to South Dublin by Mrs Warwick's son-in-law. Hot tea, and a warm bed for a fitful end to the night.

The next day I woke up in Blackrock, in Dublin's leafy suburbs. I was to stay in Blackrock for most of two years, until the end of Senior Freshman year at Trinity, commuting into the university by train.

How did the fire start, you are asking? It turned out that the lodger from the top floor, the one who thankfully had roused me from sleep, had a history of arson.

Mountjoy Square

"Mountjoy" denotes "prison" for many Dubliners. But for me it meant the opposite: freedom, independence, maturing, and becoming my own person.

This was because four of us single male students moved into a flat together in Mountjoy Square. We did not buy any pot plants. Our record was seventy-six empty milk bottles, which we could not be bothered returning to the local shop. My bedroom window was permanently stuck open at the bottom after a recent coat of paint – very pleasant in the summer for a cool breeze, but glacial in winter months when a chill blew round the Square.

Male students tend to be like cats. Independent, going our separate ways, coming alive at nights. Rarely did we feel the need to communicate our whereabouts to each other during the day. Into the wee hours, though, we would talk at length, Paul the most extroverted one serenading us with his guitar and latest musical composition.

We did invite visitors at times, and invariably they were served our "special" dish. Our *pièce de résistance* was Vesta curry and boiled rice from a packet, followed by chopped banana on a delicious bed of butterscotch whip. Looking back, I remember we even had the temerity to invite our favourite lecturer and her husband to dinner at our flat, but at least they had the privilege of partaking in our special meal too, and the good manners to eat it all up!

The story would not be complete without an admission that some of our flat's residents regularly visited the single girls' flats for a square meal as opposed to a Mountjoy Square one… where they ate surrounded by flourishing pot plants.

An added attraction for me was that Heather was one of the occupants of that flat. We had agreed during the summer before university, after a great summer working and hitch-hiking in Scotland, that we would be best separating emotionally for a while, as our relationship was becoming too intense and all-consuming. We needed to study, after all! However, since we attended the same Modern Languages lectures, we could continue to be friends. I plunged into French literature; Heather's diary became crowded with people to see.

Summer jobs

Trinity terms were short, a mere six or seven weeks of intensive study. Then, the yearly examinations were held in September, which spoiled a totally uninhibited and joyous summer, but the majority of us made the most of our freedom in July and August anyway.

Modern Language students headed for the Continent, ostensibly to brush up on their French, German, Spanish or Italian, but really to have a good time while hopefully improving their language skills as a by-product.

The choices I made were these:

- Waiting on tables and general kitchen dogsbody in Hôtel Rosât, Château-d'Oex, canton Vaud, Switzerland;
- Volunteer at a Christian Movement for Peace work camp in Bouxwiller, Alsace, on the French border with Germany;
- *Moniteur* in a children's *colonie de vacances* in the *Massif Central* near Le Chambon-sur-Lignon, in France; and
- A month at a summer *Ferienkurs* in the university of Heidelberg, Germany.

None of the job experiences above destined me for greatness, but they provided plenty of invaluable opportunity to understand and appreciate differences of outlook and culture, as well as to view first-hand some beautiful places.

For the summer course in Heidelberg, Robin and I lived in a *Birkenhaus* - a cabin made of birchwood – in the grounds of a bungalow at the top of one of the steep hills, which overlooked the picturesque German town far below us. Robin was a fellow occupant of the Mountjoy Square flat. In those youthful days, we had the energy to climb up and down this hill morning and evening, giving us time and space to absorb and assimilate the complicated German lectures we had attended in between.

The Hôtel Rosât's location was equally magnificent. When off duty, fellow Trinity student Derek Johnston and I could relax, and allow our eyes to drift across the valley from our balcony, over the green fields and lower slopes, to where a setting sun painted the mountains pink in the pure Swiss air.

It was on that summer vacation job that I learned to eat peanut butter and jelly (jam to me) sandwiches from our American volunteer workers, and to drink the occasional spiced hot wine in the village café. Non-alcoholic, apparently.

We staff climbed up the hill behind the hotel during the night, to see the sun rise over the mountains at dawn. At least, that was the idea – some of us didn't quite make it to the summit. While resting in a disused log cabin on the way up, *something big* made its way round our shelter with a loud crashing noise. Convinced it was a wild bear – are there tame ones? – we made good our escape, and were soon back in the safety and comfort of our châlet beds.

More successful were the hitch-hiking competitions we held. We each had a day and a half off per week, and the aim was to get as far as possible away from the hotel, while arriving back in time to resume work.

Derek and I did well on this challenge. We each managed to reach Italy and return within the thirty-six hours. My journey was more straightforward than Derek's. I managed to reach our target youth hostel before dark, and slept soundly. He found himself close to target, but couldn't find the hostel in the darkness. He slept on straw in a convenient barn, only to discover, when daylight broke, that the hostel was a matter of yards away.

Derek regaled us with stories of his exploits on these days off, as only Derek could. Perhaps the funniest was the time he was pursued around a ruined amphitheatre at night-time by some dodgy Italian men. He had definitely chosen an unfortunate place to spend the night *al fresco*!

Europe

Apart from the summer jobs and courses, we Christian students often joined forces to serve on teams in Europe. Baptist teams to Brussels were popular: they lasted two weeks, and forced us out of our cosy comfort zones, as we were required to go from door to door and engage with the local folk in French. Likewise, we sang and took turns to testify inside the church.

I felt most vulnerable in such circumstances – speaking publicly in what was not my mother tongue. But it stood me in good stead for when Heather and I participated on Gospel Literature Outreach teams later on in the north of France. There we gave testimonies in French, and spoke in the open-air, with (usually pleasant) hecklers having fun at our expense, and skate-boarders whizzing past our noses as we were holding forth. *Ah, zee Freench. Zhey do zings differament, non?*

Mentors and tormentors

Gordon Dalzell was about ten years older than we were; his

wife Helen was closer in age to ourselves. They have become life-long mentors and friends.

To have mentors who are half a generation older is ideal, it seems to me. Near enough to remember and appreciate your stage in life, old enough to be potentially wiser! Yet the input that this particular couple have had into our lives is so rich, that I almost hesitate to write about it, for I feel incapable of doing it justice.

We met in Dublin in the early 1970s, when Gordon was student chaplain for the Irish Baptist churches. We students enjoyed his company, ability to empathize, Bible knowledge, missionary zeal, and general *joie de vivre* and enthusiasm for life.

He possessed a somewhat cavalier approach, where it seemed as if the function of obstacles was to show how they could be leapt over. His reputation had preceded him a little: some of us were aware that he had met Helen from Gateshead in the north of England, become engaged to her after three weeks, and been married within six months. This demonstrated his decisiveness, and might have been perceived as reckless, except that they remain married after fifty plus years! There is no doubting Gordon's leadership qualities. He was chosen as Head Boy at Campbell College, at the time N Ireland's only public school. Then, for us aspiring male sportsmen, he had the annoying habit of excelling at every sport he attempted to play. He had played grass hockey for Ireland, and after not lifting a golf club for a year, could very well shoot under 80 – not bad for a very part-time golfer! He had our admiration though.

Gordon came into my own life at just the right time. I have described the episodes of depression in Hereford, which periodically carried over into university life, so to be in the company of a man with pastoral gifts, and a zest for life, changed my inner well-being so often in the short term, and my outlook on future years in the longer term. For above all, Gordon was an encourager for many of us in the Irish university scene in the early 1970s.

Later I'll write about the 'Jaunts' and trips to the continent, but to jump forward a couple of years, when it was time to leave university and join the workaday world, Gordon was a powerful influence. All I wanted to do at that stage was become a light-house keeper. Seriously! I had looked into it as a way of escape from people, where I could live happily in isolation, though helping folk from afar on the high seas!

My mother and Gordon had other thoughts. Mum sent me the advertisement for boarding master at Cabin Hill school in East Belfast. This was the preparatory department for Gordon's old school, and the post included teaching Latin and French to boys of between eight and fourteen years, and coaching the hockey and cricket teams. Apart from the sport, the idea of the rest of this job filled me with dread. Imagine having to get up every morning, to address, persuade, teach and control a class of boys, many of whom had no desire to learn languages? Without external encouragement, I would not have applied. With encouragement, I did so and was offered the post, one of the best career choices I ever made, as it forced me to come out of the dark cave I had retreated to inwardly.

A few months into teaching, I asked to see Gordon and Helen to discuss another matter. They had been aware that my relationship with a very fine Christian girl from Belfast had ended. A little while later, Heather Best had returned from her year in Germany, and was completing her final year at Trinity. Her own lengthy relationship with a Christian surgeon had recently finished too. He had been older, about Gordon's age, and my prospects of a renewed relationship with Heather were nil for some time. But here was an opportunity for me to step in again with an offer of closer friendship! Did my mentors think this was wise, after so many ups and downs since the age of fourteen, when we had first met? Were we as incompatible as Heather sometimes imagined?

"We think you should go for it!" was the advice they gave, perhaps not in those words, but certainly in the subliminal message. They had separately had some access to Heather's current aspirations and relationships, so had more insight than most when it came to putting one lively, people-oriented young lady together with one serious young man on the verge of retreating into the solitude of his man cave for ever. Risky on all sides then. But that was Gordon's way. He enjoyed calculated risks. As mentors, he and Helen saw the potential in their 'tormentors', and for our part, we knew that they were in it for the long haul. The relationship they had started with me and others they intended to continue for as long as the Lord kept our paths together, and even beyond that.

Which is why, even today in my mid-sixties, I still value and cherish visits to the Dalzells in Cambridge for a mental, spiritual and emotional MOT.

Jaunts with the Dalzells

Gordon bent over the dining-room table, his tall lean frame silhouetted against the light from a small table lamp.

"We could all meet up somewhere round about *here*," he said with a long finger pointing towards the middle of the spread-out map of Europe. "Now we just have to find a suitable campsite..."

Invariably, the jaunts to Europe began with the germ of an idea, the idea took hold, caught fire, and spread among us Christian students in the universities and colleges of Ireland. Many of us were language students, and needed little excuse to head off to France or Switzerland after our third university term was over, and the holidays stretched ahead.

Knowing that such jaunts would include good fellowship, and often trips to *L'Abri* where Francis and Edith Shaeffer had established their community, made the ideas even more attractive.

Gordon needed little encouragement, and was in his element when masterminding these trips to European destinations with groups of students. Transport wasn't a problem. One or two old campervans, hitch-hiking if there wasn't sufficient room, boat and rail for some – one way or another twenty or thirty of us would congregate at a pre-determined location.

One such was the campsite at Aigle, nestled at the foot of a steep Swiss hillside. This allowed us a daily commute up to *L'Abri*, where we listened to taped Christian speakers on all manner of subjects: Biblical Psychology, Art and the Christian, Faith and Philosophy. We had the privilege of attending open question-and-answer sessions, where Francis Shaeffer himself would enter, climb on to a stone fireside perch, pull his legs clad with walking breeches up under him, turn to his expectant audience, and announce: "Well, who's first?"

Whereupon, we were all free to pose any and every query we had about the Christian faith, how it applied to society, life, or the Arts. He was equally at ease with theological questions, and listened carefully and with respect for all, whether they were young or old in the faith, or even sceptical non-believers. It was most impressive, and a learning experience with lasting impact for us hungry students.

Back at the campsite in the evening, our physical hunger was satisfied too. Meals were simple but healthy. "Luxury on Less" Gordon would later describe his and Helen's philosophy to me, and we could readily see it in those halcyon days too. Muesli, peaches, plums, yoghurts, Swiss cheeses – whatever was in season and for sale at good prices in the local *Migro*s supermarket. We ate well. Then with full stomachs, and happy recollections of the day, we would sit around in small groups and pray for the world, with information supplied by – you've guessed it – the Dalzells. China regularly featured, as it was close to Gordon and Helen's heart.

When the jaunt was over, we were sent off two by two, not to evangelise, but to find our way back home to England, Ireland or wherever home was, as best we could. We felt we were the privileged ones as we set off hitch-hiking. The short straw choosers had once again to brave the perils of travel in the old campervans, which had managed to reach Switzerland after an adventure or two, but were now definitely well past their sell-by date.

Recreating the vibe

It was fun to return to France in post-student days with Gordon, Helen, and their daughters.

Joanne and Charis – their two eldest - had had a whale of a time on jaunts with the students: they had so many willing playmates. Now school teachers and without children as yet, when July arrived Heather and I were free to travel with the Dalzell family down the length of France to the Midi. True to form, we camped with our red Toyota Hiace van and tents under shady fir-trees and acacias in Port Grimaud, and rubbed shoulders with the rich and famous of an evening in St Tropez just round the coast. Luxury on less. There we cast an admiring but not envious eye at the yachts and cabin cruisers pulled up at the quays, so that all could see their affluent occupants sipping champagne and cocktails on deck.

Heather was brought down to earth next day on the campsite, when the very handsome and personable North African toilet attendant asked her out on a date. She admitted to being somewhat flattered, but resolved that from that day on, she would never venture forth without her wedding ring on! In that part of France on the beaches, the practice is to wear as little as possible. After a few days, Heather and I remarked to each other, that the less a person wears, the less they communicate verbally. It is as if scantily clad people need to protect themselves somehow, so they withdraw into themselves. It is certainly easier, we found, to talk to a stranger when they have their clothes on...

Our most recent attempt to recreate the Jaunt vibe was a stay in a farmhouse in the north of France with Gordon and Helen. This was upmarket accommodation, complete with swimming-pool and *haute cuisine*. They also offered bicycles for us to explore the flat roads and lanes, and the beautifully kept military graveyards of Picardy, a real treat for all four of us.

But this did not really live up to Gordon's maxim of Luxury on Less. It was just luxury, plain and simple. Or, at least, a step up from the Jaunts. It revealed to us just how soft we had all become.

Edinburgh

I have always had a soft spot for Scotland.

Perhaps it is there in my genes? My father's family hails from the Scottish Borders several centuries ago. So I'm happy to consider myself an Ulster-Scot, but my mother went and complicated things, as her family came from the Cavan Monaghan area, which is almost the Republic of Ireland.

When it was a question of choosing a college for Teacher Training, therefore, Moray House in Edinburgh won hands down. This choice was made primarily because of the location and the city, rather than any in-depth study of curricula or teaching methodology.

In spite of a rather ordinary presentation of modern language teaching methods, I never regretted the decision. As my elective course for the year, I chose Outward Bound, which qualified us to take groups of children into the great outdoors for adventurous experiences. However, first we had to go through fire, wind and rain ourselves, to show the world that we were personally capable of the various feats.

It was a great excuse to have a lot of fun. As a group, bonding was swift as we sailed dinghies on Linlithgow lake, learned how to sub aqua, walked and froze in the Scottish hills, or got lost together as we orienteered. The highlight, though, was a weekend in the Lake District in the north of England. There we abseiled, and attempted to claw our way up increasingly difficult rock faces.

We went from "Easy" to "Severe" in one jump. It was the greatest physical challenge I had ever met up to that point in my life. I recall looking down after only a few yards' climb, to see my fellow apprentice shaking his head, and giving up there and then. And he was a well-built rugby player. Sobering. I determined to keep on looking up, a parable for life really.

There were parts of that climb where you had to abandon your foot and hand-holds, commit yourself to swinging across a gap, while pretending you were not what seemed like hundreds of yards above *terra firma*. Well, the rock was *firma* enough, but also very *perpendiculara*. Funny the things that go through your mind when you are in extremity. I took a deep breath, and committed myself to crossing the gap. The fact that I'm writing this shows that I made it across.

What stands out from the experience was the elation we all felt as a group that evening, in the warmth of a local hostelry. Glowing faces in the firelight. Muscles where I never knew I had them. Pectorals to die for. Well, at least not to be ashamed of.

Edinburgh city seemed so solidly Scots, with its upright

citizens, its upright maroon and cream double decker buses; its rocks, castle, houses and facial features chiselled out of granite. Arthur's Seat, Princes Street, the Scott Monument, the Woollen Mills, Jenners, the Usher Hall – the landmarks all became so familiar to me, as I walked past them and up the Royal Mile almost every day. In the end I was sorry to leave.

It was great to connect with believers in Ferniehill, a small and lively Brethren assembly which attracted many students. 1976 was an exhilarating year for many of us, as we were on the verge of new lives, and new careers. There I made friends with two Northern Irish lads, Stephen Hagan and Desi Hamilton, both students at Edinburgh university. They met and subsequently married Linda and Morag, two lovely Scottish lassies, and settled down in Orkney and Crieff respectively. It has been intriguing to follow their families' progress over the years. Stephen took over Linda's family farm in Westray, and ended up as Convenor of the Orkney Islands Council. While in Edinburgh, Morag lived in the "Mish", the Edinburgh Medical Missionary Society, where I also roomed. In her downstairs flat I met Sally Magnusson, who became a TV presenter.

My teaching practice was at Heriot's, the private school, followed by Musselburgh Grammar, and finally Greenhall High School, a comprehensive secondary. This gave me a sampling of both mixed gender classes, and single-sex ones, of excellent teachers and others who struggled, so that I was gradually able to decide how and where I wanted to practise, what style would best suit my personality, and so on.

All this was invaluable and purposeful, as was my long train trip down to Aberystwyth during the course of the year.

Heather and I got engaged at Christmas 1975, and planned to get married in August of 1976. Well before then, however, she had already booked her teacher training in Wales, and for me to reach her required a trip of many hours in those days.

She remembers me bringing down my dirty socks to be washed (by myself). For my part, I recall sitting in on one of her Modern Language teaching classes, taught by Carl Dodson, whose Bilingual teaching method had become renowned. The basic principle was to have as many small interactions and repetitions between teacher and student as possible in the target language during one lesson. I almost felt I learned more in one hour than I had in three terms up north, but of course this was just my personal perspective.

So Heather and I were now ready and willing and eager to communicate our pearls of wisdom to unsuspecting French and German classes in Belfast and district. Heather started out at the Girls' Model Secondary School; I travelled to Lisburn to teach at Wallace High School.

For my part, I saw that it was not only our future students who were in need of instruction. Heather and I were about to get married. The sock episode had taught me that I also needed to learn a lot about how to live closely with a lady, and learn quickly. Our perspectives on life were so different. With hindsight, I perceived that it might have been more appropriate to arrive in Wales with a bunch of flowers, rather than a case full of dirty socks. These days they call it life-long learning.

Teaching

Armed then with the latest language teaching methodology, and with memories of observing very competent teachers fresh in my mind, I embarked on what was to be four years of teaching French, German and RE in Wallace High School, Lisburn.

It was September, 1976. Newly married on August 18th and just back from honeymoon on Cumbrae island off Largs in Ayrshire, Heather and I started out in a gate lodge in East Belfast, near Parliament Buildings, Stormont.

Early each morning, Heather would travel with some other teachers who had a carpool, and head across town to the Girls' Model Secondary School in North Belfast. The Troubles were at their height, so these journeys were not always straightforward. My route was easier: I would join two other Wallace High School teachers, and head west, to the town of Lisburn.

Experience in Cabin Hill, and on teaching practice, helped me understand that to be a successful teacher was not about wowing the pupils on the first morning of the school year, but about how you managed the full year with all its vicissitudes. What the students learned over the course of the whole year was more important than one's own reputation as a teacher. This longer-term thinking and perspective was most valuable preparation for our future career in the marathon that is a Bible Translation project.

Wallace proved to be a pleasant place for both students and teachers, and the environment was conducive to learning. For my part, there were a few principles that I tried to adhere to, probably not rocket science, but it kept both me, and I hope the students, alert.

The first one was to keep as many students as possible engaged during the forty minute slot I had with them daily. For this, no one activity should last too long, and there could be half a dozen different ones per lesson. Progress in language learning required ability to listen, understand, and respond orally. It also required skill in writing and analysing language structure, and knowing how to correctly manipulate the forms of nouns, verbs, adjectives. All the above needed to be included and kept in balance.

The second principle was to recognise that students assimilated language in different ways, partly reflecting their temperament, but also according to their preferred learning styles. So each new topic had to be introduced with this in mind, giving the visual learners something to see, and the auditory learners something to listen to! If the two could be linked, so much the better. If there could also be an element of surprise and unpredictability, so much the more memorable. For some ideas, I had our Psychology lecturer at Moray House to thank. I loved the way he arrived in one day, and threw a toy black crow at us, which flapped its way threateningly round the auditorium. He also asked us to bring our bags and cases to the front, while he proceeded to place blank white sheets of paper along the rows where we sat. Because of conditioning, we experienced fear and apprehension in both cases! (because of Hitchcock's film "The Birds", and then normal exam procedures) These particular gimmicks I never tried on my students, but I always remembered the point he was making, and the power of the unusual in teaching!

I was privileged to teach in Wallace at the same time as a number of gifted teachers, many of whom went on to become Head teachers: Harry Morrow; Ian McCallan; Raymond Pollock; Bill McGaffin; Bobby Jennings. David Manning was a senior pupil when I began teaching, and became Head of Strathearn school when our daughters Joy and Rachel were later completing their secondary schooling in East Belfast.

Early days of marriage

In a word, these were great!

There was an overwhelming sense of a fresh start. We had left the family units which had nurtured us so well, and were now starting our own little family. This was very freeing, and at twenty-four, we imagined we were ready for it.

In some ways we were. Heather and I had known each other

for ten years, on and off, so quite quickly, we were both able to look forward in the same direction, rather than spending too much time on introspection.

Brooklands Gospel Centre, where we had settled to worship and serve, was an ideal arena for many young marrieds who joined the fellowship in and around 1976. A Young Marrieds' group was created for mutual support, and many friendships formed then persist to this day.

Heather and I threw ourselves into the Young People's work, with Teen Time on Friday and Youth Fellowship on Sunday nights. This was tiring after a busy school week, but rewarding to get to know young folk from the Ballybeen estate, who told you what they thought of you in no uncertain terms. Being Sunday school teachers, we went as helpers to camps on the Isle of Man, which opened our eyes to the way of life that these young ones were accustomed to. So often, their background of the survival of the fittest would mean that they would start camp on the offensive and defensive, but those barriers would come down, and they became relaxed and affectionate in a stable atmosphere of trust. It was wonderful to witness life transformations only God could bring about.

Training

Heather had been more than a little bit shocked during my wedding speech, when I announced categorically that we would be going into Bible Translation. I guess she hadn't quite grasped that it was definitely part of the "package"! In those days there were no pre-nuptial agreements with the marriage plan spelt out. "Marriage prep" – a great idea no doubt – passed us by. But even if everything might now be seen as rather ad hoc, amazingly we somehow muddled through.

However, in certain areas we were prepared. We had both attended an Introductory weekend together at the Wycliffe Centre in Horsleys Green, Buckinghamshire, during our engagement, and Heather had been very impressed and enthusiastic about the course content and presenters. "Very spiritual, but very grounded" was her description of the Wycliffe folk she met there.

Teaching was an ideal profession, when it came to taking the SIL (Summer Institute of Linguistics) courses. They ran for ten weeks during the summer holidays in Britain. Nowadays the focus is on "just in time" training, where prospective translators and linguists are fed just enough knowledge to keep them going in Field situations for the first two years, after which they return for more training, and often to write up a dissertation on their early language research.

In the "olden days", however, we students were crammed full of all the knowledge it was felt we needed for the length of a translation project! Perhaps I exaggerate, but we did leave the SIL courses with a certain amount of mental and intellectual indigestion! It is very true that some of what we learned we did not need to use until several years down the line.

Heather and I loved the training at Horsleys Green. Phonetics, Phonemics, Grammar, Semantics and Translation, Literacy, Anthropology, Exegesis. Some of this was familiar to us from our language background, but much was new, especially as applied to minority languages from all corners of the world. The South of England was warm, sunny and dry, so students could practise their exotic Phonetic sounds while lying comfortably on the grass, gazing down over the picturesque rolling Chiltern hills. Safely grazing sheep, their jaws moving from side to side, stared back in bemused bewilderment from the other side of the fence.

Cocoa time was a nine o'clock fixture at the end of a busy day of teaching and learning, when we could compare notes, and enjoy cross-cultural encounters with the many nationalities who attended the SIL training courses. Volleyball was a group game popular with all. Happy times indeed.

The Irish Baptist College

We were able to rent the gate-lodge near Stormont for our first year of marriage. In a later chapter, I tell of our quest for a house to buy. Meanwhile, we stayed with my parents in Glengormley for a time, then rented part of a house in East Belfast again, when the renovation on our new wee home was nearly finished.

The cottage in Old Holywood Road was ready by the time we left teaching, to embark on a new adventure of faith, which began with a year's training in the Irish Baptist college.

In 2019, this college is located in lovely new purpose-built premises, near Moira in Co Down. In 1981, it was in a large building on the Sandown Road in East Belfast. We now lived just a few miles away, so we made the short trip daily down the Belmont Road, past Strandtown and Ballyhackamore, to attend our classes. Baby Joy was a great sleeper, and allowed us both to keep up with lectures and studies. Moreover, the budding potential Baptist pastors were able to hone their baby handling skills at break and lunch times. Joy didn't seem to mind at all.

The College kindly allowed Heather and me to pick and choose lecture series which were relevant for our purposes as linguists and translators. So we thoroughly enjoyed further grounding in Greek and Hebrew, along with exegesis in a number of New Testament books. Thankfully, we were spared sermon preparation and presentation in front of the student body, sometimes a harrowing experience. Instead, we gave a missionary presentation on Wycliffe, which was infinitely more comfortable for us, and hopefully a pleasant change for the pastors-in-training.

And that was it. Introductory and advanced SIL courses - tick. Bible College training - tick. Six weeks in France to brush up our spoken French - tick. Barrels packed and sent ahead - tick. Assemblies and churches visited, and supporters updated - tick. Final goodbyes to family and friends – tick.

We were ready to go. But can anything really prepare you for the oh-so-different life in Africa?

Cameroon

In December 1982, we flew to Cameroon, which was to be our first experience of Africa as a family. This was where Wycliffe's Africa Orientation Course was held, designed to introduce new recruits to African life.[1]

We were now four of a family: Joy was a toddler of two, Rachel born that September was just three months, plus Heather and myself.

Douala airport was our first hurdle. It was crowded, noisy and seemed chaotic. But we had been forewarned. A helpful friend had told me that if you are having trouble getting through and have little children with you, a gentle prick with a safety pin administered in timely manner to make one of them cry, can work wonders! I guess he was saying that African officials are compassionate deep down, and do not like crying babies! Happily, I did not have to resort to this, and I hasten to add that it is definitely not Wycliffe policy.

---

[1] For a fuller account, see *No Ordinary Book.* Ambassador, 2004. 2nd Pod Edition 2015.

The heat and humidity, which everyone besides us seemed comfortable in, was what hit us first. Then the queue out to the aircraft, as we waited on the blisteringly hot tarmac, was not British. Rather, it resembled the crowd outside a superstore in the January Sales, when the doors were about to open. Yet we made it on board, and we flew in safety to the interior town of Yaoundé, which I remember as being altogether more tranquil.

First morning in Kamba village

Heather and I awoke together with a start, to the sound of loud but friendly laughter outside our window. It was bright, it was sunny, it felt good to be alive. My eyes moved slowly round, taking in our little bedroom: it all seemed much less fearsome now that daylight had dispelled the shadows.

'Mbembe kiri!' I jumped. The words had been shouted just a few inches from my left ear.

'Kiri mbung,' came the distant reply.

Ah yes, Ewondo morning greeting. That much we had learned in the capital Yaoundé before braving the village. Languages, as I said, are my passion. I come alive when I hear a new one. So, eager to get up and about learning Ewondo, I slipped on my shorts, T-shirt and flip-flops, and ventured forth.
But first I wanted to check up on Joy. I'd left her fast asleep in her cot the night before. As I looked in on her last thing, my torch had picked out one very large fat spider on the wall above her sponge mattress. Heart pounding, I had drawn off

my sandal, taken aim in the dark, and let fly. I hit the spider, and it crumpled with an amazing lack of resistance. But out of its body scurried dozens of tiny spiders! For all of five seconds I felt bad: I had just made them all orphans!

'Joy ...?' I called softly, opening her bedroom door. But her little bed was empty, the mosquito net pulled back. Rising panic. Oh no, had she run off?

'Joy!' I raced out into the bright courtyard.

'Hi, daddy!' I pulled up short.

And there was my little two year old daughter, sitting on the door-step of the adjoining hut, her giant Richard Scarry book propped up on her knees, happily pointing out her favourite pictures to our host Vincent's second wife, Marie. Joy and Marie had clearly become great pals, without a word of language in common!

'Mbembe kiri!' the courtyard called out in chorus.

Now what was it ...? Half a dozen faces were turned expectantly in my direction.

'Kiri mbung!' I somehow managed to reply.

Smiles all round. I had passed my first language test.

Macho moments

We were in at the shallow end, learning to swim in Africa. The purpose of the Cameroon orientation course was a serious one: it was designed to break us in gently to life in West Africa in a safe context, with staff keeping a caring eye on us in the background, giving occasional advice and encouragement before we headed for our eventual assignments. During village phase, we were involved in co-operative projects with the local villagers. The first was to provide a clean water source by building a concrete platform and pipe system around a natural spring of water. The second project was to help construct a village school.

But it was the personal, cultural lessons learned which stand out in the memory. There is one which I will never forget. It happened the very first day I spent in Kamba village, before we moved there with our families and baggage. We were about to have our first taste of village life, and I was part of an advance party invited to meet the villagers.

Our future hosts were showing us round the different dwellings we would inhabit for the next six weeks. The atmosphere was a happy one amongst the green recruits, as we walked in single-file self-consciousness alongside our new African friends. Ahead of me ambled our six foot, sixteen stone photographer, the group's most eligible bachelor, monopolised by a little old African lady who kept insisting that he needed a wife. I smiled at his attempts to put her off.

From behind me came a babble of excited voices, as our group rejoiced in new sights and discoveries.

Suddenly I felt someone's hand slip into mine. I froze. This could not be my wife: she was back in the city. With a swift glance, I ascertained that, yes, it was the nice young man who had been walking harmlessly at my side moments before.

I looked him in the eye. He smiled back, openly, with an encouraging nod. I gulped, and walked on. Just being friendly. Yes, right, I had heard of this phenomenon, I had even witnessed it on the streets of the capital between Africans, but I never expected it to actually happen to me! In my mind's eye, I could see the broad smiles on the faces of my golfing mates I had so recently left back home. A furtive glance over my shoulder showed colleagues too busily engrossed in their own cultural preoccupations to care. That was a relief. I decided to pretend I was enjoying myself, smile at my host, and even essay a swing to the arm as we walked on.

My mind was racing. Where I come from, men are men, we do not need to hold each other's hands to be pals. If we hold hands, it is to haul one another up severe cliff faces, to have an arm-wrestle, or possibly to engage in charismatic prayer.

I am proud to say I coped, at least on the surface, and did not offend my host. But I confess I relaxed only when, after a few companionable, lingering, fingertip moments, he eventually let go.

This was the first, but certainly not the last time that Africa brought into question my macho presuppositions. Masculine colours, men's bicycles, men's umbrellas, men don't cry ... which of these were simply cultural?

I resolved not to judge a man too quickly by trivial externals. Africa was teaching me to wait until I saw what was in his heart.[2]

Cross-cultural lessons

When one cultural background meets up with another at close quarters, there is huge potential for misunderstanding. When a group of people do things differently from the way we have grown up or are used to doing it, then our natural reaction is to attack and defend. They do it wrong, we do it right.
The chances are, it's neither right nor wrong, just different. Now even though this seems obvious, when you are mopping your brow in the throes of culture stress, it's striking how defensive you can be, and how quickly you can run to the nearest cultural ghetto which looks and feels like "home" to you.

This is true whether you call yourself a missionary, an anthropologist, an administrator, or any combination of the three. In the past, all of us have been guilty of patronising attitudes to cultures in which we have worked, so perhaps it's time we all stopped pointing fingers and got on with the business of enjoying other people.

---

[2] *No Ordinary Book,* 2015, Pages 35-38.

I like Nigel Barley's approach in his West African travelogue: *"The Innocent Anthropologist"*[3] He allows us to laugh along with him in his often unsuccessful, but funny attempts to adapt to Cameroonian culture. Humour gets him through, and we can learn from that. Then there was also a large dose of humility in his attitude: he knew he depended on the local folks for his survival, and he was determined to learn what he could from them.

Taking jiggers out of my white feet was one of the first lessons I had to learn, soon after arriving in Africa. As it happened, this was in Cameroon too. Those burrowing fleas loved my soft soles! But it was only after a week or two of vainly trying to remove the sacs whole with a needle - and re-infesting myself constantly - that I succumbed to a local teenage girl's ministrations with a piece of sharp bamboo. She removed them painlessly and perfectly each time.

It was humbling and salutary for the Western independent pride I had unknowingly carried to Africa with me, and just one of the many mistakes that littered our stay for orientation in that country, before moving on to the Ivory Coast. Fortunately, we did remember to pop a sense of humour into a small corner of the suitcase before we left.

---

[3] *"The Innocent Anthropologist: notes From a Mud Hut"*, (1983) More recently re-published by Eland Books (2011).

Ivory Coast

After surviving Orientation Course in Cameroon, we flew west and arrived in Abidjan, Ivory Coast at the end of March, 1983. Three months later, we were thrown into the deep end, and setting up home in Bahoulifla among the Kouyas, a small ethnic group of around 20,000 with a distinct, unwritten language, and a very distinct culture. Their twelve villages were scattered over a small area of rain-forest, on the fringes of the savannah grasslands, in the centre-west of the country. This area was to be our base and place of ministry for the next fourteen years.

Hey, the Chief's wearing my pyjamas!

You see, I had been sent out two pairs. One olive-green, the other light brown. Very smart they were too, with darker green and darker brown trimmings. Overly adventurous colours for me, being a departure from my customary blue or grey, but just about acceptable in the bedroom.

I had tried the green one on first. Unfortunately, whatever

material the pyjamas were made from they did not 'breathe' sufficiently in the heat and humidity, so I could only wear them on the very rare cool night. The brown pair stayed in its clear plastic cover.

Until, that is, it was time to visit the chief, after a long absence from the village. What present could I bring him? I thought around and finally decided on the brown pyjamas. Our chief was growing frail now, and would appreciate the extra warmth at night. So Heather and I wended our way down the village through the courtyards, and were very cordially received by the old chief, as he sat in the shade of his veranda, clasping his carved walking stick between his knees. On this was a 'Jesus' sticker. How he had got the sticker, we have no idea!

We went through the protocol, so familiar to us now we could do it in our sleep. A gourd with practically non-alcoholic palm-wine was passed around the group: participants blew away the surface flies before taking the customary sip. It was sweet and not unpleasant to the taste. The conversation was free flowing and enjoyable. Heather and I felt pleased with how much Kouya we could speak and understand now.

Just before leaving, we gave our present. Always gracious towards us, he accepted the gift with delight on his wrinkled brown face. The pyjamas would suit him, I thought to myself.

I had imagined I would never see the pyjamas again, for obvious reasons. But I was wrong.

One day, I was driving in Vavoua town close to the *Préfecture*, where the *Préfet*, the area's principal administrator, had his offices. This was where the suits, shirts and ties congregated in the town. And who should cross the road in front of me, heading for the Préfet's office with a retinue of our Dema brothers, but the old chief. I rubbed my eyes in disbelief. He was sporting a panama hat, and one very smart pair of brown pyjamas, with an unmistakable dark brown trim!

Then it dawned on me. We had not explained what they were for. Our gift to keep him warm at night had become his Sunday-best suit!

The linguist's dream

Well, true, one does dream of discovering some exotic suffix or fantasy phoneme one day in your adopted language of study. But a more modest aspiration would be to learn to speak a language so well, that you are taken for a native speaker.

In France, when I speak French, the French think I'm Swiss. When I speak German, Germans think I'm Swiss. I've nothing against the Swiss at all: I like them. But when I speak either French or German in Switzerland, the Swiss think I am French or German, or else an Irishman who can't speak either very well. But in my defence, I was once taken for a German by a German farmer who picked me up while hitch-hiking from Denmark. Mind you, it was he who did most of the talking on the journey. Still, I'll take it and add it to my encouragement file.

Now when you are learning a language like Kouya, you are at an obvious disadvantage here. I mean, you don't look like a Kouya, and you never will, no matter how hard you try.

However, on one memorable occasion, I was taken for a Kouya, of which I am immensely proud.

Some Kouya friends took me to a village I had rarely visited one evening as dusk fell. Walking towards the chief's house, we exchanged greetings in a number of courtyards we passed through. We sat down in some for a few moments, as was the custom. After a few moments of conversation in which I had participated, one old man enquired rather loudly. "Whose son is this?" He was talking about me. My friends laughed and explained who I was. He had taken me for a Kouya.

I was chuffed. The man was old, but he was also blind.

Consulting the mouse

Down through their history, the Kouyas have been very mobile. When faced with a problem or conflict with an outside group, their solution has often been to pack up and leave. Even internally, when a family or clan has been at loggerheads with another, one clan has generally opted to put space between itself and the other faction. The country has been big enough, the forest thick enough, for the twain never to meet again.

Now although proud of their own language and culture, Kouyas are not shy of adopting customs which appeal to them from other ethnic groups. So during their travels, they have picked up an eclectic mix of traditional practices.

One of these is the practice of consulting the mouse. They got the idea from the Mandé peoples: Yaouré and Gouro practise this also to this day.

What happens is this. A large calabash, or a clay pot serves as home for several captured mice. Normally they live on the ground floor of the pot, but an upper storey has been fabricated for them by means of a slim horizontal piece of wood, which divides the pot into two. On this piece of wood are arranged smaller pieces of wood and small stones. A hole in the middle allows the mice access to the upper storey.

In the morning, when it is time to consult, village or clan elders will gather round the calabash, open the lid, and drop some breakfast in for the mice on to the floor of the first storey. The mice stretch and yawn, and pop up through the hole to break their fast.

As they shuffle about, they knock against the twigs and stones, causing these to be rearranged. They finish their meal, then disappear down below.

Peering down into the gloomy interior of the pot, the elders then try to discern whether the day's omens are good or bad. If portents are bad, they may decide that no work should be attempted in the fields that day!

We felt that many Kouya customs and practices could with great profit be incorporated in the culture that we grew up in in Britain. This was not one of them. We did feel sad that so many for so long have consulted the mouse for guidance and direction, instead of the One who created the mouse in the first place! Yet was it so very different from those in our own culture who consult horoscopes, and whose lives are ruled by the stars?

The petrified pig

The pig eyed me doubtfully. He had been bound hand and foot, and bundled unceremoniously into the back of our estate car. I have to confess I shared his hesitancy, but I had had little choice.

Earlier that Sunday morning, I had picked up the preacher, his wife and little boy in town. Hardtop road for a few kilometres, then on to the red dusty track that led to Gatifla, a tiny Kouya village. Often we would stay in Dema, but that day we were on our way to encourage the handful of Christians in Gatifla: they had few visits from outside speakers. I drove slowly through the potholes, but had to accelerate over the rutted corrugation. A risky business. Too fast, and you were off the road: too slow, and the jolting broke your back. Over high rocky outcrops, slewing through sand, we finally broke through the bush into a neatly laid out village.

A few final bumps, and we stopped. The service was already underway, inside a house. We were offered seats at the front, facing the little congregation, where they could have a good look at us. This was not a culture for shy retiring types.

Twelve years on, it was all so familiar to me now. As I entered into the praise, and took my turn to lead in song and in prayer, I reflected on how the Spirit had been at work among this previously resistant people. Twelve years ago, this small sitting room could have held all the known Kouya Christians with room to spare. Now, it was the smallest Kouya congregation of any! God had not forgotten them after all. As one young woman sang out a line, and we all echoed it back to her, I felt the tears come. In this part of Ivory Coast, the locals say that men's emotions are in the soles of their feet, that they take a long time to reach our eyes. But something in her voice, the way she threw her whole being into the words of worship, and the accompanying mouth-organ just slightly out of tune, that's what set me off. I knew then which choir I would head for in heaven: it would have to be the Kouya one ...

Ah yes, I was telling you about the pig. Well, it belonged to Henriette's granny, a nice little old lady who had been at church too, and she was very kindly sending it (with me) into the town Mission for her daughter's family. Henriette's mother that is. Henriette herself is most persuasive, and had caught me in a moment of weakness. I had just been treated to a bowl of rice and catfish after the service, and was feeling magnanimous. So off they went to fetch the pig, plus a chicken and some freshly dug yams.

The pig and I gave each other one last lingering look, and off we all set. We took away much more than we went with. We went in order to encourage, we returned laden with blessings. And two extra passengers, as it was such a waste to have two empty car seats.

It was not a very long journey, but if *you* were bound hand and foot, and lumped into a car-boot when you'd never been in a vehicle before in your life, *you* probably would have done what our pig did! Not in protest, you understand, but in abject horror at what was happening to you.

Later, as I cleared up the aftermath, I reflected on the roller-coaster highs and lows of this life we had chosen. Celestial choir one minute, petrified pig the next. But at least we had fulfilled our mission on that Sunday morning. We had gone, we had returned, and we had not got stuck in a rut. There were days when a rut seemed the most attractive place in the world to be stuck in. But that Sunday morning, in spite of the incontinent pig, it struck me afresh that I was very, very happy.[4]

"Big Canoe's Break-up on Water" – Acts 27 in Kouya

As we mentioned, most Kouyas live hundreds of miles from the coast, in the rainforest area of Ivory Coast. Many, therefore, have never seen the sea. The only waterways in the Kouya area are small rivers, which become a mere trickle in dry season.

So the apostle Paul's sea voyage to Rome, with its storms, shipwreck and detailed nautical vocabulary, which Luke records for us in Acts 27, presented a few unique challenges for the Kouya translation team.

---

[4] Three of the above stories are from *No Ordinary Book* 2015, Pages 181, 202, and 206.

The only boats the Kouyas knew were their canoes, but this word could not describe a large ocean-going vessel. We toyed with a transliteration of the French "bateau", but settled on the equivalent of "big canoe" to express "ship". The captain of the ship became the "driver of the big canoe". The sailors? They were the "big canoe's belly working-people".

New terms had to be invented. We had to ask ourselves: what is the function of this piece of nautical equipment? So, what does a life-boat do (verse 30)? It saves people. Our term had to include this aspect, so it became a "rescue baby-canoe." In Acts 27:13, the mariners drop anchor, another concept foreign to the Kouyas. The word chosen had to describe what an anchor does: it became the "big canoe stopping-metal."!

What was remarkable was that, eventually, the Kouya translation team was able to find satisfactory equivalents for all the terms - concrete and abstract – that it encountered in the New Testament, even though some, such as nautical terms, were initially so foreign to them. We marvelled at the flexibility of this language: once the concept was understood, a way could be found to express it.

To illustrate, here is a word-for-word translation of Acts 27:12 in Kouya. First of all the English version:

"Since the harbour was unsuitable to winter in, the majority decided that we should sail on, hoping to reach Phoenix and winter there. This was a harbour in Crete, facing both south-west and north-west."

Now the Kouya word-for-word:

"But the canoe-stopping-place had not been adequate during the cold-coming-time. For this reason most people said to leave there and try to park the canoe in Fenisι. This was a canoe-stopping-place on a land-in-the-midst-of-water called Klɛtι, the face of which was towards both-sides-of-the-setting-of-the-sun. There they would sit down during the cold-coming-time."

In this verse, several Kouya words sometimes had to be used, where a single English word sufficed. The opposite was also sometimes true: one Kouya word might require several English words. But that's another story.

Learning is for life

Learning was always two-way during the years we spent living in Kouyaland.

True, we had some knowledge to impart: we had had the privilege of growing up in the Bible; we had spent years studying languages and linguistics; we had some rudimentary medical know-how.

But in many ways we felt we received more than we were able to give. We marvelled at how the Kouyas handled emotional conflicts; how they took time to grieve the passing of loved ones, and understood the necessary steps in that grief. We observed how they were transparent about disagreements and talking them through, even publicly between man and wife. We admired the warmth shown to children, and how they looked out for others' children as well as their own, even rebuking where it was needed if village children were unruly. This reflected their care and concern for their own extended family, their clan, and the village community. Then there was the value of taking time with and for others; the need to be quiet when visiting the sick, just to be present alongside to help recovery.

In all this, and much more, we realised we were amateurs in many ways.

There was the funny side of their pragmatic approach too. Their use of a Tefal non-stick frying pan for the church collection, for instance. Or the formation of a church matchmaking committee, to put one and one together. They were so good at making do with what was available. We wrote home to our parents about this committee:

Kouyas are much more up-front about matchmaking than we are. During the Christian conference, the session-leader might ask the group: 'Who here is unattached? Which men? Stand up! Which women? Stand up! Who wants to be married? Men? Women? On your feet!' Everybody has a good look around them, and there is much hilarity. We now have a Matchmaking Committee (seriously!) in Dema church, and I really think we qualify for membership: we are just waiting for the nod. Do you think we could introduce these committees to churches in Britain??

Horsleys Green

A hamlet off the A40 between High Wycombe and Oxford, Horsleys Green was for more than forty years the home of British Wycliffe.

The campus had been previously used as a camp school for disabled evacuees from London during the Second World War, and from April 1947, an all-boys boarding school was established on the site. In 1971 it was acquired by Wycliffe as a hub for Bible Translation in the UK.

Set in rural Buckinghamshire, the grounds were extensive, surrounded by beech woods, and ideal for quiet study and research, or long rambles in the forest. It was located in a Green Belt, so further building was restricted.

Heather and I trained or taught here for four summers, 1979-1982, learning the necessary skills for analysing unwritten languages and translating the Bible into them. Literacy courses showed us how to develop practical alphabets, and construct reading books. The Wycliffe principle of "study a course, then teach it" meant that we found ourselves teaching Phonetics,

Grammar and Semantics in 1980 and 1982, before we left for our field of service in Ivory Coast.

The Saunders family stayed in or near Horsleys Green for two extended periods after that: during 1985-6, and 1992-4. The first was to enable Rachel to regain her health, and the second to give Heather more recovery time following her ectopic pregnancy.

We all enjoyed living on centre. The girls had plenty of friends, both those permanently based in Britain, and translator families passing through or, like us, based there for a year or more of furlough. Life could stabilise in this environment, there were good Primary schools nearby, and a number of supportive local churches – for us Long Crendon Baptist Church.

We drove all manner of vehicles, as we had to watch our bank balance carefully! The most memorable in 1986 was an ancient mini-cooper, whose bodywork had not kept pace with its great engine. A Wycliffe colleague kindly offered us his flat for a holiday in North Berwick near Edinburgh in Scotland, and as we drove up on the M1, the fresh fall of snow on the motorway was clearly visible through parts of the car floor. Our girls took such things in their stride: to be sure, snow was a novelty to them.

Back on base, throughout that year I regularly drove the mini down to Reading university to complete a Masters in Linguistics. The dissertation was particularly helpful for our Kouya work. Called "The Kouya Enigma", it attempted to clarify the position of Kouya in relation to the other Kru languages in the chain, classifying it by means of some linguistic comparison with neighbouring languages Nyaboa and Bété.

One particular photo in our album stands out from this first period in Horsleys Green. It is of our wee family, four members at the time, with Joy aged five and Rachel three. We are all smiling in true missionary family fashion, seemingly without a care in the world. The photo does not betray the anxious time Heather and I had passed through that very morning, when Rachel had disappeared and it was several hours before we found her. It was all systems alert on centre, searching everywhere on campus, trying not to fear the worst. Being situated beside deep woods, the danger of abduction was real.

Rachel and her wee friend Andrew Crozier were eventually found on the other side of the busy, and dangerous A40 road to Oxford. They had wandered off through the forest, picking blackberries. What a relief!

Nostalgia

My brother-in-law Paul is fond of saying: "You know, even nostalgia isn't what it used to be!" Please allow me to indulge myself for a bit.

The majority of men, when you ask them to list the cars they have known or owned, will go all misty-eyed and even emotional, especially when they remember their first ones. This should in no way threaten their WAGs. We have this attraction, nay obsession in a different box or compartment in our minds you see, and as someone has pointed out, these boxes do not touch one another. We go there, we open the box, we enjoy the memories, and after the experience, we carefully close the box again.

Do skip this part if you like. The vehicles listed below came in many hues. Sometimes I'll give the colour, just to keep some folks with me. Suffice it to say that if they ever matched our outfits, it was completely accidental.

The Morris Minor convertible: this is my earliest memory of a family car. Of course it did not belong to me, but to my parents. In the early 1950s, we owned a grey Morris Minor with a fold-down canvas roof, ideal for Libya, where we lived. To close and open said roof, there were no electrics to go wrong, but I don't recall how long it took to do this manually.

Late 1950s: Black Hillman Minx. Nice family car.

1960-1970: Vauxhall Cresta. A wonderful vehicle, all the rage at the time. I saw an identical two-toned one on the road recently, heading for a vintage rally, and my heart skipped a beat. It was maroon and grey as ours had been, had bench seats and a steering column gear lever. Ours seemed massive to me growing up, but the one the other day seemed just medium-sized.

I learned to drive in Hereford, as soon as I was allowed to, at seventeen. My driving instructor had a Ford Escort, one of the first, with dual controls. I only recall him using these controls once, memorably. That's why I am still alive and writing this.

My father was very generous with me in letting me drive his cars. Looking back, I wonder would I have been as trusting? So thus it came about in the 1970s, that I had the pleasure of driving his Humber Sceptre, his Rover 2000, then his Rover 3500. He even let me take his Talbot Horizon to France with Heather, after we were married. Oh sorry, those vehicles were respectively silver, turquoise, cream and deep blue.

And now to the cars I have owned jointly, firstly with my sister, and later with my wife. Probably out of respect for his own cars, my father bought Pamela and me a grey Ford Cortina – I think the earliest model - while we were doing our studies. This one somehow took me safely to Dublin and back, when I sat my Final exams at Trinity in 1974. Out of necessity, I learned lots about what happened under the bonnet of a car (or didn't!), while in possession of this car. Many of us young ones drove old bangers about in student days. For instance, Heather's brother David had a grey Wolseley Mark 1 which he threw around the roads of Co Armagh at breakneck speed. The roads were emptier then – just as well.

In 1976, I got married. At this point, it is important to re-state that none of the following cars were a patch on my new companion in life, but you know, I liked most of them *quite* well.

Stephen, another brother of Heather, kindly lent us his light blue Fiat 127 to go on our honeymoon. Both were memorable, so much so that we were led to buy another Italian job. We purchased a red Fiat 127 as the first car of our married life. It was great while it lasted – the car I mean – but began to rust fairly quickly in our Northern Irish climate. So we went abroad, and lived in the centre of Ivory Coast, far from the sea and corrosive salt. There the Vavoua to Daloa road pummelled and shook our cars, and I developed a new admiration for Ladas and Toyotas, the former so very solid if unexciting, the latter lively and able to dance over the surface of the mud tracks. Toyota spare parts could be had all over the country, a real advantage.

Missionaries are resourceful and generous for the most part. We lent and borrowed our cars for furloughs, or forced home leave, and even shared vehicles in the cities and towns, for economy's sake. The list of Peugeots and Renaults I drove is too long to mention, but pride of place must go to a Nissan Double Cabin. This was bought for us by a generous supporter, who probably took pity on us. I regret telling our car stories quite so graphically during furlough, but nevertheless the Double Cabin was a wonderful provision for our little growing family, and all three girls were able to enjoy it. Well, Hilary was only a baby then: we bought the vehicle shortly before she was born in Abidjan.

The night of her birth was memorable for many reasons. After midnight - exhausted as men are following childbirth (!) - I was stopped by police on the empty streets, having apparently not halted but gone through a junction in this vehicle. Now the fourth of Heather's brothers, who shall be nameless (but it was Andrew), was out visiting us at the time. He was a great practical help with the new baby around, but I was to learn many years later from the man himself, that he had also been a great help in getting the police to release us. He had slipped one of the policemen some financial encouragement when I wasn't looking.

We missionaries had a policy not to dish out such rewards, so as per usual I had been quietly attempting to talk my way out of trouble: "My wife has just given birth, Monsieur. Pardon, pardon. What languages do you speak? Where exactly is it you come from? Ah, I have a colleague who lives quite close to there..." You get the idea.

After twenty minutes, they reluctantly waved us on, and quietly triumphant, I turned to Andrew and explained: "All it requires is patience. Speak even a few words in their language and it works wonders!" My passenger nodded in the darkness. I was pleased; he seemed to be growing in his cultural understanding. Little did I know!

On this happy note, though tempted to continue, I feel I should close part one of *Cars I have Known and Loved.* And apologise for any remarks that might be perceived as sexist.

Belmont Park

In 1997, the five of us returned to N. Ireland, a move which had been planned because Joy and Rachel had reached the age where they needed to join the school and university system in the homeland. The Kouya translation was well advanced, and could be completed by trips out to Ivory Coast from here on.

During those years when I spent many hours in the attic in Belmont Park, poring over draft manuscripts of the Kouya New Testament, it was vital to get out and about sometimes, to gain some perspective on life. Sometimes, I just took a trip on the train into the heartland of Northern Ireland, and eavesdropped on folks' concerns...

Overheard in a coffee-shop in Ballymoney

"I'm really worried," said Agnes. "About Jack."

Madge drew her seat closer, though everyone else in the shop was too busy with their own conversations to want to listen in.

"What's the matter with him?" she asked her friend, gently.

"He's just not 'at' himself. Moping about the house. No interest in life. Only goes out if he really has to. You know what I mean?"

"I do. And it's hard on you too."

"Yes, we women just can't detach ourselves when others suffer, can we? Anyway, that's what's wrong with me the day. It brings back sad memories too. My Charlie was just the same before he went. And it looks like the same thing to me. It's the diabetes Jack's got, I'm sure of it. Eats nothin'. But never stops drinkin'. An my Jack never was a drinker."

"Have you gone to see about it?" asked Madge.

"Aye, we have. I took him to Dr Hines yesterday. Lovely man, isn't he? Told him what I've told you. How Jack was losin' all interest in life, an all. But sure Dr Hines could see that by how quiet Jack was. Hardly a peep out of him the whole time!"

"So what did he give him for it, Agnes?"

"Well, it's the tablets they give you now, Madge. Thank goodness you don't have to have injections any more. That would have been really depressing with Jack the way he is."
"It's hard. It's hard. But look, I'll be thinking about you. I know people say they're more trouble than they're worth. But you

get attached to them don't you? And Jack's had a good innings. Well here, I need to be off, Agnes. Don't fret too much."

Agnes looked up mournfully at her friend.

"I'll try. I suppose what you say's true, you do get attached to them. And they say thirteen is a good age for a cocker spaniel. I really will try my best to be brave about it!"

(Names changed to protect canine anonymity.)

Oxbridge

With a mixture of paternal pride, and fatherly concern, I watched Rachel climb the steps to the plane taking her to her interview at Cambridge.

She reached the top, then turned to wave at me through the window of the airport lounge, before disappearing.

I felt gratitude as well. Here was our wee daughter, who had been so ill in Ivory Coast at the outset of her life, now an independent and intelligent young woman, perfectly capable of making her own way in life. Well almost, I thought, just so long as she got on the right plane...

I sat down again in the café, surreptitiously wiping away a tear. My mind went back thirty years, to Hereford. My teachers had put me in for the Oxford entrance exam, which for the first time students were able to sit in their final year at school, rather than wait until after they had finished their A levels. I had taken it rather half-heartedly for two reasons: revision for it interfered with the freedom to enjoy a summer holiday, and I knew that Heather and other Irish friends would be applying for Trinity College, Dublin. I missed my Irish friends.

However, I had been called to Oxford for interview, my first experience of the city, and I remember looking out over the city spires from a small garret room at the college, and thinking: yes, if I had tried harder, this kind of ivory tower life would have been attractive. Was I sorry? Not really. It lent itself to study, certainly, this academic cloistered life where every stone seemed to ooze history. Yet, it evoked a certain claustrophobia in me too, and Dublin called.

Rachel rang the next day, to say she had been offered a place at Trinity Hall to read English, subject to obtaining the requisite results in her A level exams. She was excited, and we were delighted for her.

So this meant Heather and I had an excuse for regular visits to beautiful Cambridge, with the wide open spaces of the Backs of the colleges, bridges over the Cam River, tourists mingling with students trying their hand at punting. For me, it had the appeal of Oxford, but without the claustrophobia I remembered. We were able to stay with our good friends Gordon and Helen Dalzell, as Gordon was pastor of Rock Baptist church in the city.

We knew that, just as plants thrive when planted in the right environment, so Rachel would flourish here, and that is how it turned out, both in relationships with a wide variety of students, and the constant academic challenge which she rose to. She was to meet Andrew Forster, an Engineering undergraduate from Peterborough, fall in love and marry him soon after they graduated. Their wedding was in St Andrew's the Great, a city centre evangelical Anglican church which they had attended during their years in Cambridge.

One very amusing incident sticks in my memory. It was 2001, and Rachel was about to start university. I was in Horsleys Green with the Kouya men - Emile, Didier and Kalou Ambroise – busy with the final checking process before the typesetting of the Kouya New Testament. Our drive up England and over to Ireland by ferry coincided with Rachel's arrival date at Trinity Hall, so we brought her with us, along with her suitcases.

City centre parking in Cambridge is limited. And this is how it transpired that Rachel's grand entrance to Trinity Hall for her academic career was marked by an elegant, blond young lady leading the way for her African bearers, who were carrying her bags and suitcase up on their shoulders, in true Kouya fashion!

Perfectly natural for the Kouyas, very slightly embarrassing for Rachel. For me following behind, what was hilarious was that no-one in Cambridge batted an eyelid.

Meanwhile, back in Belfast...

Forte

Ballroom dancing, I decided, was not my *forte*.

I had suspected this all along, as I am a free spirit when it comes to most things, so I knew that dancing in pre-ordained patterns would probably not be my *thing*. But I prided myself in being a dutiful husband, open to change and new ideas, so when Heather suggested we try an evening dancing class, I reluctantly agreed.

This was one of her few unfulfilled ambitions in life, she explained. Did it have to include *me*, I wondered? Sure I have friends with feet two sizes smaller, who are much more physically co-ordinated. I was certain they would be willing to substitute for me?

But no, the scenario in Heather's imagination definitely included me, so off we traipsed for our first ballroom dancing class.

It was held in the gymnasium of Ashfield Girls' School. Acoustics were terrible, varnished floor creaked and squeaked, and the portents were not good, somehow, as a motley crew of couples lined up opposite our dancing instructor.

He was a dapper wee man, immaculately turned out, fluid in every movement, and wearing shiny patent shoes. I have never liked patent shoes. He was not the kind of man who would reach the top of my ratings list, but at least his voice sounded masculine enough.

As he and his lady assistant showed us the moves, the squeaky protests from the gym floor drowned out their explanations. But they made it look easy enough, so we budding dancers took to the floor with gusto.

In such a situation one cannot help but compare. So looking round, as one does, assessing styles and abilities, I perceived that I was not the worst dancer present. A tall chap in massive white trainers, bent almost double, was clumsily dragging his tiny partner round the floor like a two year old in a supermarket. Oops, Philip, concentrate on what you are doing! I was happy to see that Heather was really enjoying herself, and actually very good at this lark. I relaxed a fraction.

But the lady assistant was looking around, I think, for vulnerable males needing remedial help. At one point, our eyes locked. Mine said: "I'm OK." Hers said: "You're not OK." And so it was, that at the next pause, a few of us were whisked away from our rightful owners, and told where our feet should go. I watched with a mixture of emotions as Dapper Dave commandeered my wife, and disappeared into the sunset in a whirl of smooth wiggles.

To cut the story short, I do not take criticism very well, and my new partner delighted in doling it out. Every ounce of dancing dexterity and confidence drained away from me, and I was left a wet rag.

Heather has never really understood why I never returned to dancing class. But by means of a bribe on the quiet, I persuaded our youngest daughter Hilary to take my place that next week. And furthermore, call me a coward if you like, I made sure that my translation trips abroad coincided with every possible future dancing session at Ashfield Girls' School.

It's not a real language, is it?

"Wir fer gan hame noo. Eftèr kirk an aa, tha weans ir hungrie got."

"Aa richt. Wull see yis oniehoo afore tha nicht's oot."

Heather and I turned and looked at each other silently, eyes widening. What was that?

We were parked at Benone beach on the North Coast, after church on a fine Sunday in summer. Car windows were down to catch some breeze, when two cars pulled in, one on either side of us. Their occupants began to call out to each other, oblivious of the two linguists between them.

And so we were treated to several minutes of Ulster-Scots, the very first time we had heard it spoken between what were obviously native speakers. Of course we'd been used to listening to the brogues of Ballymena and Coleraine, but those were clearly varieties of the Ulster English we knew and loved. This was different, unlike anything we had heard before – and we had grown up in N Ireland. We were intrigued, and wanted to find out more.

We knew of the existence of Ulster-Scots. We had first been contacted back in the mid nineteen-nineties by the Ulster Scots Language Society. They had wanted to start a Bible Translation project. Could we help facilitate it? At that time, though, we were heavily involved in the Kouya translation in Ivory Coast, so we were not free. Yet we kept the idea at the back of our minds.

Then in 2003, we were approached again. By that time, the New Testament in Kouya had been published. Our family home was in Belfast.

Translation in Ulster-Scots was ready to roll. Some funding was available, but most of the work would be done by volunteers, Ulster-Scots speakers who would give freely of their time. So we arranged some seminars on translation principles for a wide group of interested folk, following which three small translation teams formed, working in Newtownards, Cullybackey, and Greyabbey. The Ards peninsula, County Antrim and East Donegal were the principal areas where the language was spoken, mostly in rural, farming communities.

We were all of us working part-time, just when we could. The translation started in earnest in 2006. Three years later, Ulster-Scots Luke was published, entitled *Guid Wittens frae Doctèr Luik*. The teams then tackled the other three Gospels, and saw reward for their efforts in 2016, when *Tha Fower Gospels* appeared in print.

These two publications were the product of many happy hours spent in the company of fine Christian translators, as we wrestled together over choice of appropriate words, phrases and register. What kind of translation should it be? There were options in choice of words. There were plenty of very antique Scots words, some of which we were prepared to use, if their meaning was clear from the context. But besides being accurate, reflecting original Greek, we also wanted the meaning to be clear, and the style to reflect the Ulster-Scots spoken in Ireland currently, so it would be accessible to both young people and older folk too.

We were often asked: 'Why bother with such a translation? Is it not a luxury? Don't we already have enough Bibles in English, which most Ulster-Scots speakers can read and understand?' Well yes this was true, but for us it was and is important to preserve ways of speaking, and we knew that translating the Bible was a fantastic way of doing this, and of opening up languages to the world. And then, with the creation of the Digital Bible Library, that world was to become even more accessible - on laptop, tablet and smart-phone.

There was one other very important reason why we saw a translation into Ulster-Scots as highly desirable. In Wycliffe our mission is to reach the peoples of the world in languages that speak to their heart. We have seen folk reduced to tears - good tears! - as they have listened to sometimes very familiar verses read in their own heart-language. That is the effect and impact of Scripture translated in a new, fresh way.

Here's a wee snippet from Luke 21 (verses 1-4) in Ulster-Scots:

Tha weeda wumman's offerin

1. Jesus lukt up an saa tha weel-aff fowk pittin thair offerins intae tha kïst ïn tha Hoose o God.
2. Then he saen thïs puir weeda wumman drappin ïn twa pennies.
3. "A'm tellin yis tha truith," qo he, "Thïs puir weeda haes gien mair ner onie o tha rest o thaim.
4. Aa these yins hae onlie gien a pïttance oot o thair pruch intae tha kïst, but thïs weeda, puir an aa that she ïs, haes gien aa she haed tae leeve on."

The main translators became good friends, and many a happy day was spent in the company of Elizabeth McLeister and May Kirkpatrick in Cullybackey, and Bill Currie, Philip Robinson and Sally Young in Greyabbey. A number of other folk – too numerous to list – made excellent contributions too, as the translation was drafted and honed.

Castlerock 3

The Good Morrow (1592) by John Donne

And now good morrow to our waking souls,
Which watch not one another out of fear;
For love, all love of other sights controls,
And makes one little room an everywhere.
Let sea discoverers to new worlds have gone,
Let maps to other, worlds on worlds have shown,
Let us possess one world; each hath one, and is one.

(verse two, italics mine)

I have always felt that this chapter deserved a separate book, and it may yet.

At one point when "fun's wuz low" – money was scarce – Heather and I toyed with the idea of spending a year in our wee studio in Castlerock. Amongst other tasks, I would enjoy writing up our experiences, under the title:

"CRAMPING MY STYLE"

A year of marital bliss
in a room and a bit

A year we have never managed. However, we have succeeded in spending a day, two days, or a week here and there in one of our favourite places, and one of our favourite seaside villages. Here are some diary entries from 2015.

18th August, 2015 - Down the drain

The day got off to an inauspicious start. And really, there was no reason why it should not have been auspicious. Today is after all our thirty-ninth wedding anniversary, and we were celebrating it in beautiful, in many ways unspoiled Castlerock, on Ireland's North Coast.

Usually, we are only able to come up here for a night or two, such has been the itinerant nature of our work and lifestyle up until this point. Now though, we had promised ourselves longer stays in the studio over coming months. Peaceful days and weeks stretched ahead of us luxuriantly.

I have hinted that the day did not begin well. Before nine o'clock, a knock came to the big window at the front of the studio. We stirred. After a few seconds, another knock, this time on the door. No, I wasn't dreaming, there was definitely a real person there, knocking. Some context is necessary. For one, we never get anyone calling here at the studio, ever. Secondly, Castlerock does not wake up before nine in the morning, and we have gone native in this respect whenever we have stayed here.

So it meant either that someone had died in the family, and the police were informing us, or I had parked badly and was blocking someone from going off to proper work.

After some moments of fumbling and knocking over furniture, I opened the door. It was our neighbour Don, from the studio round the front. He's not a policeman, and I have never seen him irate, so that was encouraging.

But he was the harbinger of bad news, especially on one's wedding anniversary, and more especially at the beginning of our mutually agreed new life of confinement, where there was nowhere to go: our one studio room was *it*.

"I'm afraid the drains are blocked, Philip," he said.

As I tried to take this in, he continued:

"Mine are okay, round the front. Water's running away there, but you see these four man-holes here..." Don turned and pointed to them; they were a couple of metres from our front door, parallel to the front of the studio. "We can tell that they're full, about to lift their covers..."

"Don't know where the blockage is. Last time, we got the Department of the Environment out, and they unblocked it with rods and such, but said it was not really their job as it was not the main sewer. Next time we'd have to hire someone private. The blockage could be right under the flats, under your studio and the one next door."

Practical problems of this nature do not excite me. Nothing within me sees them as a challenge to be gloriously overcome, especially not before my first cup of coffee in the morning. But give me my due, I was very polite to Don, discussed the problem rationally, and accepted his kind offer to return in an hour, when we could together lift the manhole covers, and view the sewage for ourselves.

I closed the door, my heart in my boots. Heather had only heard snippets, and once she had ascertained that all family-members were alive and well, had buried herself back under the duvet. Isn't it amazing how modern women can be so fixated on masculine and feminine roles when it suits them, I thought? But I dismissed this as uncharitable: it was, after all, our anniversary.

The story of our first day up north could have been disastrous, but I am happy to report that it wasn't. After an hour, Don and I rolled up our sleeves, took a very deep breath, and opened the manholes. Numbers one, two and three were full, as he had forecast. Number four, though, was mercifully empty. That meant, even to a mechanical slow learner like myself, that the offending blockage occurred between three and four, and not somewhere under the building. Excellent! Armed with gloves and broomhandles we set to, and to our joy, all of the offending material, which I have been at pains not to describe as it is not yet past the watershed, gushed on its merry way through hole four, and away down under the block of flats. Gone! Jimmy came from Bertha's bar to see what the craic was. I imagine Bertha's will probably feature a little in this year's journals, if "things get bad". Jimmy is good at clearing up messes it seems, and had a hose which he unrolled and brought up to us, so that we could do a real good cleaning up job on the sixteen visible pipes we had just uncovered.

Don went away saying he'd a mind to tackle some of his other longstanding problems today, because luck was with him, and he was on a roll. As for me, I whispered a prayer of thanksgiving, and put it down to divine intervention, and the fact that it was our thirty-ninth wedding anniversary.

19th August, 2015 – Private space

Heather and I have come up from a two-storey detached chalet bungalow, with two reception rooms, kitchen, two bathrooms, three bedrooms, and a study each. Where we are now living together is a studio flat, comprised of one biggish space six metres long by five metres wide, with a tiny utility room leading on to a shower room, with small basin and ordinary sized toilet. The larger room doubles – no - trebles as kitchen, living room and bedroom.

There is one large window and one door, both looking out on to the car park with numerous manholes, a park used by flat owners like ourselves, and visitors to Bertha's Bar, which you can access either from the back here, or if you have no shame, from the front.

So for a couple used to rattling round a big empty house now that their three daughters are happily married and away, private space in the studio is at a premium. There is only so long you can linger in the toilet without arousing suspicion of being anti-social.

We came up with the obvious solution. We have a heavy curtain which may be drawn across the main room, to make the bedroom a separate entity. One person can therefore do their own thing whilst enjoying the living room and kitchen, while the other one lies in bed doing *their* own thing. There is unfortunately no extra space in the bedroom part to do anything else but sit or lie on the bed itself. But it is amazing how human beings can adjust to that, and happily read, type, speak or talk on their mobile phone while lying prone!
This then is how Heather and I hope to achieve our private space when we are here. When the curtain is pulled across, we promise not to communicate - except in dire emergencies, such as needing another cup of tea or coffee.

Right now, though, as we stand (or lie), there is a real advantage to having the bed. For one, you can fall asleep; for another, you have access to the most responsive "hot spot" in the big room. Meaning that you can best link on to the internet from the right hand side of our bed. Other spots in the main room are cold or lukewarm at best. We know about this from our African experience: there were particular mango trees or hillocks which for some unknown reason allow a better signal.

So the right hand side of the bed is very attractive for both Heather and myself, given that we have no landline or internet connection in the studio. Fortune has decreed that in our thirty-nine years of married life (see yesterday's entry), the situation has evolved whereby wherever we are in the world, I always sleep on the right hand side of the bed, as one looks down towards the foot of the bed. Originally, it had something to do with my keeping my sword hand free, and Heather feeling more protected.

It seems that now, though, having managed to reach her sixties, she feels less need to be protected by me and my sword, and is rapidly claiming the attractive hot spot as her own.

20th August, 2015

When the weather is fine like today, we escape our confined quarters and head for the beach. It is only three minutes away, and we have promised ourselves a daily walk when we visit. Many walks remain in prospect then.

Soon after we hit the sand, Heather spots a stray MacDonald's cup. It took all of her willpower, and some pressure from me on her elbow, for her not to pick it up.

"I remember hearing about a woman," she objected, "who picked up ten pieces of rubbish every time she went out for a walk! She said that if everyone did that each time they went out, the world would be a cleaner place."

"You really admired that woman, didn't you?" I offered.

"I did indeed," replied Heather, with a small smile as self-knowledge dawned.

"You won't do it every time we go out for a walk together in Castlerock, will you?" I asked anxiously. Short pause.

"All right then, I'll try not to."

So I am left clinging on to an elbow, and this half-promise.

22nd August, 2015

"All real men carry cash on their person!" Heather maintains.

Is this true? I am not so sure, but many times when we go out for a walk, I am asked: "Do you have some cash on you?"

Inside, I counter with: "All real women can't pass a shop without wanting to go in and buy something!"

But of course, wisdom dictating a response of silence, I bite my tongue, like a real man.

24th August, 2015 - A life on the ocean wave

Living in rather cramped conditions means it is imperative for morale to get away from it all for a day out, and what better way than to make our way down to Portaferry for a fishing expedition out into the Irish Sea?

Long standing friends, Doug and Maureen Edmondson, kindly invited us to join them when we were in country in August.

This was a truly relaxing day which never disappointed. We originally met Doug and Maureen in Nettlebed, Oxfordshire, not far from the Wycliffe Centre at Horsleys Green. This was during our first summer of SIL in 1979. They were from Northern Ireland, so we spoke more or less the same language, which was a welcome change from mangling the tones of Mandarin, or Zulu clicks, or the rhythmic syllables of Japanese during our training course.

It is a friendship which has stood the test of time. Doug and Maureen had applied their artistic and practical skills to make a lovely home in rural England, combining the best from ancient and modern. Over the course of time, they moved to Lambourn in Berkshire, acquired a holiday home in Scotland, continued to provide lavish breakfasts to hungry teenagers in Ashbury before church, and to be generous to all and sundry. Maureen always had a cookie jar; it helped to be employed in Food Science at Mars Ltd. Some of the quality just needed to be tested in a home environment by Irish visitors with a sweet tooth.

We enjoyed visiting them when on furlough, with or without our children. Doug has managed to retain his dry sense of humour, in spite of Heather's gentle provocation and raising of contentious issues.

In time, though, they sold England and they sold Scotland, and they bought Northern Ireland.

To be specific, they bought Portaferry. And in particular, Barr Hall Barns, with its uninterrupted views across to the Mourne Mountains. Again, they completely renovated the old stone edifices, fixing them up inside and out, making part available as Tourist Board accommodation, and it has become a mecca for many.

But I digress. I wanted to talk about fishing in the Irish Sea. This has become the Edmondsons' favourite means of switching off from the high level jobs in which they continue to serve.

There was old John and young John, you see. Father and son. They lived on the sea-front in Portaferry, within sight of the harbour and their pride and joy – the *St Brendan*. This carefully maintained fishing boat of theirs could always be spotted loitering around the plush yachts and the cheeky rowing boats, sulking almost in its desire to be chugging off to sea to do a proper job.

So, especially in August, if the weather was favourable of a Monday, Doug and Maureen would arrive with their fishing rods and tackle, binoculars slung round their necks for the seals, seabirds and porpoises, and a picnic box full of goodies. Barr Hall guests were welcome too, along with any stray missionaries.

And that's how we came to be bobbing up and down and rolling with the *St Brendan* when she cut her engines, and we threw our hopeful lines over the side. Sometimes, patience was required, but who cared? We had just admired the lounging seals on the way out from Strangford Lough, negotiated the dangerous Narrows – well, it was John who did it to be truthful - and what more pleasant prospect than a few hours of sun and sea? To starboard was the Isle of Man, to port was the Irish coast. Above us fluffy cumuli skated lightly across a calm blue sky, and beneath us lurked the wrecks of shipping past, where massive cod were busy deciding which of our exciting lures they wanted to devour first.

The fish began to bite seriously. Mackerel aplenty, the odd nice pollack, some codling to be returned until they grew up, a rainbow wrasse perhaps or the surprise of a ling – there was plenty to keep us interested, with exclamations from all over the boat. We had visions of a good freezer-full to keep us going over the winter.

Old John, face weather-beaten and with a kind smile, spent much of his time unravelling the tangles of inexperienced fisherfolk; Doug lay back in contentment in the stern, waiting for "the Big One". Maureen was all action: if she wasn't landing fish, she was serving coffee and goodies from Mars to the whosoever wanted it. Heather was bravely releasing her mackerel from their hooks, while I savoured the scene from the bows, sipped coffee, and waited for the other Big One.

"All right, lines up!" shouted John. "Or we'll miss the tide back in!" Reluctantly but obediently, we began to reel in. "Who caught the most?" "Och, no contest!" And so the friendly banter continued as we headed West and homewards.

Uncannily, clever Doug in the stern always seemed to wait until the last minute, before landing a big cod. We joked that it took one to know one.

Boat tidied up, mackerel filleted, gannets and gulls stuffed with fish-heads thrown to them, all too soon it was time to climb the barnacled steps and up on to the pier, to where people were clean and curious as to what we had caught. Driving home as it grew dark, it was a job to stay awake in the heat of the car, and it took a good week before that distinctive fishy smell disappeared.

But then again... who cared? Friendships were renewed. Freezer was replete. Faith in the joy of living was restored.

26th August, 2015

The discerning reader will notice a short gap in this journal.

I have an excellent excuse. We had the excitement yesterday of hearing that our youngest daughter, Hilary, had started into labour nine days early! Happily we were nearby, and not abroad somewhere, so we tarried by the stuff in Bill and Hilary's house, and began the anxious wait by the phone. About six hours later, we heard from Bill. All was well, baby Zoë Elizabeth Foye was born safely, and labour had been short and intense.

All this happened in Craigavon; Castlerock is not the only place where important events take place.

So Heather and I were able to visit Zoë with her new mum and dad this afternoon. Wonderful: so fragile, so perfect. It was quite a party, with four grandparents, an uncle and aunt with their two children, and a close friend all visiting.

Within four months, then, we have received the gift of two grandchildren: Finlay, through Joy and Tim; Zoë, through Bill and Hilary. We look forward to getting to know them as they develop and grow.

27th August, 2015

As our train pulled slowly out of Great Victoria Street station in Belfast, I was in reflective mood. Plenty of thoughts around for the ninety minute ride.

I was chewing over the expression: "There's no gain without pain." And another, somewhat related one it seemed to me: "A spoonful of sugar helps the medicine go down." What was the connection, I wondered? Well, things that are hard to stomach are softened by something sweet, and if you are striving for something worthwhile, you might have to endure some suffering in order to accomplish it. Pain and gain – seeming opposites – are linked.

The train picked up speed as it left the city. It was obvious to me why I was thinking along these lines (no pun intended, but I'll take it). Heather and I were with our daughter Hilary and her newborn baby Zoë yesterday. For the mother who has gone through so much pain, that recent, vivid memory is softened as she cradles the newborn child in her arms. And each day of delight in the new arrival enables her to put more distance between herself and the rawness of giving birth. Tangible gain, after terrible pain. Even the balloons, the presents, the cards, the thoroughly deserved goodwill and congratulations - these all were helping her healing, and taking her that little bit further along the road of recovery. You are probably thinking that I am a slow learner in this area, and you'd be right. I imagine that most people have a natural understanding of how all this works emotionally.

What I do know is that after a visit to my dentist in East Belfast, it does me good to head for Bell's coffee-shop a few doors down, and promptly undo some of the positive work on my teeth with an Americano and an iced Chelsea bun. Two steps forward, one step back, but boy do I feel the better for it! Pain, gain, and slight loss.

And what is it about when your crotchety old aunt unexpectedly reveals a tender side? It modifies our fixed opinion of the person she is. Maybe, after all, once upon a decade, the aunt in question understood the power of just being nice.

Now what did the old aunt have to do with anything? The rhythm of the train, and the heat in the carriage caused me to drift off in the middle of these loosely connected thoughts. I could maybe write about this subject one day, I mused, if I ever got my thoughts in order...

Before I knew it, that nice lady on the intercom with the English accent was encroaching on my dreams, with her valiant attempt at the Irish place-names. "This train is for Derry/ Londonderry. The next station is Castlerock. Please mind the gap as you disembark from the train, and be careful not to leave any luggage behind you."

I alighted, minding the gap, with my rucksack on my back, and meandered along the platform to the barrier. Even at the dawdle which is Castlerock pace, it only took me five minutes from there to reach the tranquility of the studio.

28th August, 2015

"To be genuinely creative you can't have all your plans 100% closed, as the story hasn't been written yet and I don't want to limit the magic of what might happen." *(Marcus Robinson on his filming of Van Morrison concert in Cypress Avenue, E Belfast.)*

Well said, Marcus! Over-planning can stifle the Muse.

1st September 2015

"Philip, it's 9 o'clock. It's time you were up and about, like any self-respecting Christian man!"

"You'd better watch out, Heather, or you'll find yourself in my forthcoming book again, and today you may not appear in a very good light!"

With that, I turned over to enjoy a few delicious, final, horizontal minutes.

Such are the little minor manipulations in marriage. But I've discovered that the threat of appearing in print in a bad light is a pretty effective lever.

24th January, 2016

Sharing a small space with the one you love is idyllic, there's no doubting it. But of course it is not always sweetness and light.

She likes to have all the surfaces clear. That means table-top, bed, cabinets. *He* likes to know where things are, and that usually means actually seeing them. He doesn't want to have to search in the depths of a cupboard for the jar of coffee, or the pot of honey. He wants his shoes to be visible when he's about to go out; but she wants his size tens neatly arranged in enclosed bespoke shoe rack.

When they leave the studio, she is aware that they may never return: an accident may be waiting to happen around the next corner. Therefore the studio, which reflects her housewifely capabilities, has to be scrupulously tidy upon departure. Her reputation is at stake after all. He, however, knows that in heaven he will be so enjoying all the blessed delights that he will not care about the mess the studio was left in. Really he is the more spiritual of the two of them, as he always suspected.

Then of course, there is personality. The extrovert loves to laugh out loud at funny *YouTube* clips, just when the introvert is busy getting in touch with his inner life and reactions, in order to write his priceless prose. And then of course and unfortunately, he just *has* to know what was so funny. What an opportunity, though, to exercise those communication principles learned so long ago it seems, and regularly discarded in the hurly-burly of life. It could and should go something like this (but usually doesn't):

Him: "Honey, I'm just trying to put down a few thoughts about our relationship…"

Her: (*with sudden interest*) "Oh sorry, dear, I thought you were just looking up the rugby."

Him: "Well no, actually I wanted to explore some differences in the way we approach life. And how we can maintain our closeness in spite of these little obstacles…"

Her: "Oh that sounds great. Anything I can do to help?"

Him: *(By switching off that racket for a start)* Perhaps if you were to turn down the volume a little on the funny programme you're watching, it might aid my concentration?"

Her: "Why certainly, darling. I wasn't aware you could hear it."

Him: "That would help me immensely. You know how tricky it is to get the precise word you want sometimes."

Her: "There, is that better?"

Him: "Sorry to be such a pain."

Her: "I understand. Artists need time and space to produce their masterpieces."

Him*: (with a glance to see whether she is serious)* "Steady on! Remember it's just me you are talking about."

Her: "Yes of course, I nearly forgot. It's just you. But all Art, even the most feeble attempts, needs to be respected."

Him: *Considers this quietly. Feels he has somehow been vanquished in the battle of wits...*

Footnote: For more of the above, read P Saunders: *No Ordinary Marriage: the agonies and the ecstasies (Forthcoming: probably when we are too ancient to care or fight any more).*

My ideal coffee-shop

Well, I'm not so sure about the "ideal" bit, but my *favourite* caffeine oasis at the moment has to be *Crusoe's* coffee shop in Castlerock.

It's named *Crusoe's*, because it's run by a family called Robinson.

Here's why I like it.

You enter by climbing a rather steep flight of stairs, so there's a sense of achievement as you reach the summit, and satisfaction that you don't quite yet have to use the chair-lift provided. You turn right through a doorway, and are met with a buzz of happy voices, and some pleasant light jazz in the background.

Trying hard not to look at the luscious caramel chocolate slices, or the succulent cherry pie, I order my usual sensible panini with ham, brie and vine tomato, along with lemon water, followed by a coffee. They have won UK-wide awards as Baristas; I wasn't at all surprised when I learned that.

I pay, and look for a newspaper and a reasonably secluded seat, of which there are quite a number. I notice a few regular clients, and nod to them. The grey-whiskered retired art teacher; the young woman who slips in for some refreshment, in between school runs. Over there by the window are what looks like two earnest property people from Coleraine, brokering a deal. I can see some members of Castlerock's one long-term Chinese family, from the much loved and frequented carry-out.

All so familiar, like comfortable slippers to me.

But you know, there's always the chance that one will bump into somebody famous in a coffee shop, or someone about to be famous. Just think how many people didn't take notice of J K Rowling, as she typed away in the corner of her local café.

One balmy Castlerock afternoon, as I was sipping an almost perfect cappuccino in Crusoe's and catching up on the Sport in the Belfast Tele at the same time - who says men can't multi-task! - I happened to look up and round the busy room. At the table right next to me, sat a man who looked awfully familiar. Now where had I seen him before? This was a typical Northern Ireland moment. My mind flitted back and forth. And then it struck me.

It was James Nesbitt, the actor. Right there at the table beside me, in 3D, up close and almost personal. He was chatting away with an older man, and a lady of a certain age. Of

course, he hails from the North Coast, I remembered.
Quickly I returned to the rugby in front of me, not wishing to stare. What to do? Should I wait for my moment, then politely ask for a Selfie with him? Or should I act all cool, pretend not to recognise him, mind my own business, go about my normal Crusoe routine? Give the famous some space.

Undecided, I privately texted two of my daughters for advice. Their reply was a laughing emoji, with the advice: "Stay cool, dad!" There seemed to be an underlying meta-message: "Act your age, dad."

Slightly disappointed, I concurred. I didn't get my picture, but I did gain a little insight into the Nesbitt family dynamics, even though I tried my best not to eavesdrop.

So James left without knowing that I recognised him. For all I know, however, he was acting all cool too, and later telling all his friends that, you know, he sat beside Philip Saunders in a coffee shop, and never let on he knew who I was...

Just a couple of famous ships passing in the night, we were.

Joy in adversity

It's always intriguing to learn how couples first met each other, and how they got together.

Joy and Tim live just a few miles from Castlerock now, and Tim's family hails from Donemana, not far to the West. We see them regularly when staying in the studio, but they originally met in Ivory Coast, where Joy grew up!

Both were short-term teachers back in Vavoua International School, which our girls attended as boarders while we worked with the Kouyas.

Joy and Tim happened to be teaching there in 2002, when civil war broke out in Ivory Coast. Staff and pupils had only one hour to hurriedly pack a suitcase, store valuables, and leave in a convoy, for the rebel army was advancing at speed towards the school from the north.

Tim drove a car, while Joy kept up the spirits of the three students in the back. They passed through Daloa town, and turned east in the direction of the next big town – Bouaflé. But it was getting dark, and there was a curfew in force! What to do?

They stopped for a break in a small village. Then they heard a familiar noise. It was the sound of simultaneous out-loud praying, typical of Ivorian evangelical churches. They investigated, and to cut a longer, great story short, they were able to spend the night sleeping or dozing on the hard wooden church pews, or on mats on the concrete floor.

They were most grateful to the Lord for providing a solution to this crisis. Joy reported that they all stayed safe from harm, if not from the over-friendly mosquitos in the church.

It has often struck me that this was one unusual way to get to know your future life-partner better!

China

It seems strange, given the teeming millions in this fantastic country, but it was in China that I felt more lonely than I have ever felt abroad.

With so many years spent in Africa, as I walked the pavements of Chinese cities, I felt ignored by those who passed me by. No-one was interested in catching my eye, their focus was on the pavement, and all seemed to be intent on their daily purpose or target, and their focus definitely didn't include me.

So this is what it meant to live in a goal-oriented, non-relational society. The fact that practically all the shop signs were in Chinese characters didn't help me to feel included. "Philip," I upbraided myself, "you have known all along, have you not, that the gateway to enter and understand a culture is to start learning its language. You shouldn't be surprised that you feel awkward." I resolved to do better.

However I did get up unexpectedly close and personal with a local resident one day.

Crossing Chinese city roads was a lottery. A local friend gave me some helpful advice. "First stand on edge of pavement. Next, close eyes. Then, take deep breath, and step out boldly into traffic. Traffic will usually avoid you. Open eyes once more when reach other side."

Cars, vans, tri-shaws and bicycles did follow the conventional channels and rules, more or less, but wider roads had a counter-flow on each side. This meant that you had to look right, look left, look right again and left again, in order to reach the haven of the opposite pavement. My memorised Green Cross Code went out the window.

I learned the hard way. Which was how I found myself up very close to an elderly, shocked Chinese lady. I had stepped out from the kerb at the wrong moment. She slammed on her brakes, and next thing I knew, I was tumbling off her handlebars which I had grabbed in self-defence, apologising profusely in English with Chinese bows and gestures.

She gave me a pitying look, and rode on in her single-minded way. For a moment, I stood, still in shock. It's amazing how quickly and easily one's self-confidence can evaporate in a foreign culture.

Chinese takeaway

Take away the fine old buildings
Raze our history to the ground
Throw up piles of glass and concrete
Bleak and sad pillars of progress

Take away the joyous bird-song
Just to fill a stomach or two
Leave us with the void of yearning
Straining after fading melodies

Let us obliterate Art
Let us wipe out Nature
Let us do away with God
If we can
Chinese Takeaway

Bamboo rafting on the River Li

They woke us before dawn, and brought us down to the river
Li. Heather and I didn't know it at that point, but we were in
for one of the most memorable and exhilarating experiences
of our lives.

Mist shrouded the river bank, as we stood, shivering a little
from the unaccustomed cold, since our days had generally
been hot in China. Out on the water, ghostly figures and boat
shapes moved to and fro, with the odd call in Chinese
interrupting the silence just for a moment.

Thankfully, our hosts were confident in what was going to
happen, and we relaxed in their smiling company, following
them along a narrow path.

We came to some activity on the water's edge. From afar, it
looked like a broad platform with men on it, some carrying

long poles. As we approached, the picture sharpened, and we saw that the platform was actually a collection of smaller bamboo rafts, each with its own boatman. Other sleepy visitors stood around, clutching woolly fleeces around their bodies for warmth.

We were assigned a raft, and our cheerful hosts bade us farewell, pointing to two fragile-looking bamboo seats at the front of the boat. Heather always likes solid ground beneath her feet, but she somehow reached her seat, and sank gratefully into it. "Got your camera ok?" she asked me. I patted it in reply, as it swung safely on my chest.

The raft was composed of half a dozen thick bamboo logs strapped together, with a pleasant view of the dark calm water here and there between them. The vessel rose at the front where our feet were, and also towards the rear where our smiling, rather toothless boatman stood at the ready, his long punt half visible, half under water. He pushed downwards and backwards, and we were off, into the flow of the River Li.

Admittedly we were still half-asleep, but the whole event had taken on a dream-like quality. Punting along quietly, passing other boat shapes moving in both directions, the raft partially submerging beneath us as the pole propelled us forward. We raised our feet a little, in sync with our boatman's strokes. Gradually, the morning mist began to clear. We glided past dugout canoes here and there - with men paddling, and small black shapes on their bows. What were they? They looked like birds. Then I realised: cormorants! These were fishermen with their trained birds, straight out of the *Rupert* annual I had read as a boy.

The mist rose further, and what a sight we were treated to! Beyond the river, in the distance, as the sun gradually rose and warmed our bodies, a range of mountains appeared. Over the years, we had admired Chinese paintings with ultra-slim hills reaching for the sky, surrounded by wisps of misty clouds, but we had thought them to be simply products of a fertile artistic imagination. However, we now realised that what had seemed surreal to us, was real! And they had a special name too: they were *Karst* mountains, splendidly reflecting the first rays of sunlight that morning. I got busy with my camera.

But not for long. The river began to flow faster, and it was clear we needed to pay attention to what lay ahead. I glanced back at our boatman, who looked supremely confident. The silent river Li had begun to growl beneath us. Frighteningly. Again I looked back. Our punter had raised his punt clear, and was motioning to us to hold tight to our bags and each other!

There was no going back now. Ahead, we heard screams. And increasingly loud splashing. We were heading rapidly for a weir, we could see it ahead now! And over the top we went, dropping, dropping, clinging on to our shaky seats and to each other, lifting our feet when the front of our raft went right under as we reached the bottom. Slowly, all too slowly, the bows of our boat floated up before us, and we were again drifting serenely on a calmer stretch of the River Li.

We have a photographic record of the event. I didn't take it, but some entrepreneurial local folk did. Our boatman brought us over to their shelter on the bank, and they were already busy laminating a picture of us looking terrified, mouths open, as our raft tumbled down the weir.

We were still alive, and out of gratitude for that blessing, we paid through the nose for a picture of the evidence that we had survived.

Waringstown

I was fifty-five when we moved as a family to live in Waringstown, which was for Heather a return to the place of her childhood. Her parents' first house was on the Banbridge Road in the village, and now we were living in Tudor Lodge, just a few hundred yards down the road.

It seemed Heather knew practically everybody, or their mother or grandparents. The following story, which Heather wrote and which I have sneaked in when she wasn't looking, shows the web of inter-relationships typical of the Lurgan district.

Unexpected blessings at Bannfoot

"And that's Esky schoolhouse where your great-grandmother and her brothers and sisters received a good education." On down the long straight road to the Bannfoot we drove, to the village of Charlestown, where the River Bann flows into Lough Neagh. We stopped for a few minutes to admire the quiet beauty of this lonely place.

Many a time my husband and I would come down here in the late afternoon when the fading light has that special quality and we are sometimes treated to the sight of a single lonely swan making her silent way towards the great expanse of the Lough. Now we wanted to introduce our daughter Rachel and her husband to this part of the world, after all her years of living in England, so we made our way down Memory Lane one Sunday after Christmas. Having spent most of her childhood in West Africa's Ivory Coast, Rachel was eager to be reconnected with her roots.

We travelled along Derrycrow Road and stopped near the old tumbledown cottage where her great-great-grandparents had lived, overlooking the Lough. Rachel's husband Andrew was amazed that we were familiar with all the homes in which these previous generations had lived. We could take them not only to our own former houses, but those of her grandparents, her great-grandparents and now to the humble ivy-covered cottage of her great-great-grandparents.

 "And that's where your great-great-grandparents worshipped," I remarked some minutes later, pointing out Bannfoot Methodist Church.

The stained-glass window which proclaimed, 'I am the door' had always puzzled me in childhood. Why would a window say it was a door? I hadn't yet learned about the Seven "I am" statements of Jesus in John's Gospel.

"Oh, there's a light on in there!" Rachel exclaimed. I glanced at my watch. Three thirty. Time for the afternoon service. "How about it, shall we join them?" Rachel and her husband Andrew nodded enthusiastically. Our spur-of-the-moment decision was to bless us richly.

It was 'flu season and numbers were sparser than usual. But in the beautifully simple building, the Rev Spence had prepared the service for the dozen people there as carefully as he would have for hundreds, and the four of us, all singers, swelled the volume of the little gathering.

After the service a lady came over to Rachel. "Were you the wee girl who was poorly in Africa?" she enquired kindly. "Yes, I was." "Well, we used to pray for you all the time. We went to the missionary prayer meeting in your Grandad and Grandma's house every month, and we always prayed for 'wee Rachel.'" Rachel and her husband were deeply moved. Molly Wilson, someone they had never met before, had offered up prayers for Rachel more than thirty years previously, and they had been graciously answered. What a precious moment!

It was strangely moving as we sat, to think that Rachel's great-great-grandparents had worshipped there, that her great-grandmother had sat in these pews until her marriage, and that her grandfather and her uncle, both Methodist local preachers had preached there on many occasions. We looked up at the stained-glass window in memory of her great-great-grandmother Eliza Jane Turkington and thanked God for the priceless heritage of genuine faith and commitment to Christ filtering down through many generations.

*"Lord, you have been our dwelling place throughout
all generations."*
*"Teach us to number our days, that we may gain a
heart of wisdom."*

Psalm 90

Eating humble pie

"Should I take the points and pay the fine, or just sit the course?"

"Take the course," Heather advised.

Yes, I had joined the ranks of the many caught by a speed camera. Racing along at thirty-seven in a thirty miles per hour zone. I sighed and agreed.

And so it was that I found myself sneaking into a public office building early one morning, and sitting in uncomfortable silence with a bunch of other miscreants.

I thought I knew a few things about driving and road etiquette, but the course surprised me by revealing much of which I was unaware. Nevertheless, when we were asked to confess our crimes, the room was full of excuses and self-justification. A nurse returning home exhausted after night-duty on deserted city streets; a youth who hadn't seen the 30 mph road-sign; an older lady late for church.

For my part, I thought: "I love that car of mine. It seems sad in third gear. How can they expect me to keep below thirty miles per hour in fourth gear, on a wide and empty road? What about those motor-bikes that burn up our road at eighty after dark? Where are the police and cameras when those bikes are about?" Yes, I was definitely in the group of self-justifiers.

With great patience and wisdom, our instructor listened and then shared with us a series of pictures of car accidents at twenty, twenty-five, thirty, thirty-five, and forty miles per hour, showing us the damage to both vehicles and people who had got in the way. For all in the room without exception, seeing the injuries suffered by the children hit home hard.

So even though I avoided the driving points, I certainly got the point of the course. There are good reasons why we need to hold back, and stay within the limits.

Nostalgia revisited

My life-long love of cars is becoming obvious again. I said I'd eventually come back to the car theme, and this seems like a suitable point to do so.

Does it seem to you that cars have faces? Or expressions? To me they do. Some look pleasant, some look innocent, others are poker-faced and you don't know what they are thinking.

The Vauxhall Cresta we owned in the 1960s had a permanent broad smile on its face, displaying its chrome teeth.

The Standard van my uncle Frank owned at the time bore a mournful expression, like a spaniel's, in contrast to its owner's cheery personality. Uncle Frank would extinguish his dashboard lights at night, and pretend to us children that we were going a hundred miles per hour. Somewhat reckless without seatbelts, if truth be told, but great fun. I imagine he never really took us above fifty.

The Austin 7 had a cute little oval grill to complement its cuddly round shape, which gave it the nickname of "Baby Austin".

These days, cars' front grills tend to be more bland and same-ish, but there are exceptions. The Alpha Romeo wears its number plate on the side, like a smirk – enjoying being different. The Mercedes, while it always had a prominent badge above its bonnet like the Rolls Royces and Bentleys, seems to be getting a bit full of itself latterly: its emblem seems to expand on its grill every time a new model is introduced.

Madagascar

or: Have you ever seen the like?

The island of Madagascar is over 1000 miles (1580 km) long and 350 miles (570 km) wide. As such, it is the world's fourth largest island, and lies on the western fringe of the Indian Ocean. It may be close to Africa geographically, but culturally it is a million miles away in some ways. The original inhabitants, it seemed, were intrepid mariners, and sailed across from Indonesia in the East following prevailing winds and currents, bringing their language and cultures with them. Apparently, the closest relative of the official Malagasy language outside of Madagascar is Ma'anyan of southeastern Borneo.

Numerous books have been written for travellers about this unique, exotic country. Countless films have been created documenting the wildlife: Richard Attenborough's series on the flora and fauna of Madagascar explored the island's treasure-store – with an estimated 80 per cent of species indigenous to Madagascar, and found nowhere else in the world. What was remarkable was that these programmes totally captured the interest and imagination, while there were only rare glimpses of human beings, despite the island's 25 million inhabitants! The latter are just as interesting!

These millions speak close to 20 languages between them, and as I have only begun to explore one of them – Tanosy – my colleagues who live on the island more permanently can provide a much deeper analysis and understanding of the linguistic and sociolinguistic context than I can.

So what follows below is my own simple 'take' on what is a fascinating linguistic and ethnological mix on a breathtakingly beautiful South Sea island. What I have to say is based on a dozen short visits to the island of a month each time.

First Impressions

The Malagasy are small of stature. With my six-foot frame, I regularly felt like Gulliver among ultra-pleasant Lilliputians as I interacted with them. For photographs, I had to duck and weave, to stop my head being unceremoniously chopped off (by the camera, I hasten to add). For this reason, it is unlikely that I will ever be mistaken for a Malagasy, however hard I try to acculturate. A second drawback is that my ears are too big by far. Sit behind a collection of Malagasy friends, say in church, and you are struck by how small and neat many of their pairs of ears are. By contrast, mine are large, soft and somewhat peach-like to the touch. Yet every cloud, as they say... and it's true that my children in time past, and now my grandchildren love to play with my ears, and for the life of me it seems like a harmless pastime, unlikely to produce one of those complexes psychologists warn about.

Where was I? Oh yes, in Madagascar. The Malagasy are also active and energetic, constantly on the move. Maybe some sit under mango trees all day, but I never witnessed it. As a result, they are slim and trim, and with their eastern features, a handsome race. Looking down from the balcony of one of their tall, narrow town houses, you saw streets full of men, women, youths and children hurrying along in both directions, riding bicycles, pushing carts, carrying loads on heads, busy, always busy.

I was impressed with the variety of food on offer on the roadside stalls of Antananarivo. Up at 4000 feet on the central plateau, potatoes can grow alongside rice, bananas and peaches or strawberries. So, crops which normally flourish only in temperate climates intermingle with tropical produce. Our group of consultants witnessed this first hand, when our travel guide took us on a long walk through the paddy fields outside Antsirabe, a large town directly south of the capital Antananarivo, though still at high elevation on the plateau.

When the weather is kind and the rains arrive on time, the lands produce well, and the people flourish too. Yet as a country with one of the world's lowest incomes per capita (nominal GDP estimated at US $405 in 2017), they are heavily dependent on their crops succeeding.

Tourism boosts their economy, and is potentially a tremendous resource. They strike you as a very welcoming and inclusive people, which helps put you at ease. The town of Antsirabe itself was founded in 1872 by Norwegian missionary T.G. Rosaas, and Scandinavian influence is still very evident in the tall narrow spires of much church architecture. The

Norwegian Lutheran Mission was one of the earliest Christian missions to serve on the island, having arrived in 1866, just fifty years after the London Missionary Society began their work. Europeans in general were attracted to Antsirabe by its cool climate and the healing properties of the area's many thermal springs. It became a spa town, and over the years has known deep and lasting friendships develop between Malagasy and Norwegian residents.

Every day in Madagascar, I would see something I had never witnessed before in all my travels. I tend to be tuned in to birds, butterflies, animals, fish, reptiles and natural phenomena like rock formations, rivers, and shore-lines. But even I with my scanty knowledge of trees, plants and shrubs could not fail to marvel at the pleasure the Creator must have taken in inventing such an array of delights in all of these species.

Then the Malagasy are a musical people. They love song and dance. As you wander through a suburb of town by night, it is common to pass a young minstrel strumming his guitar, and singing to the whosoever will listen, just for the fun of it. No cap thrown down to collect tips, no damsel on any balcony that I could discern, just a joy in music for music's sake.

During the first workshop I attended in Antsirabe, the group of translators, consultants and staff held a musical evening, which turned out to be a revelation to a newcomer like myself. It was an impromptu talent show, where the cook or the groundsman, the translator or the administrator forgot the status of their day job, threw off their inhibitions and plunged into performance, entertaining us all royally. Such an unforgettable evening! I was astounded at the Malagasys' natural grasp of close harmonies, with their swaying bodies perfectly synchronised with the sometimes very complex rhythms. Our consultants' performance of *Molly Malone*, and a rendition of the Dutch National Anthem seemed all too tame in comparison, but they were graciously received as our contribution to the festivities.

Sure we were doing our best, and participation was everything.

Checking Tanosy in Toulear

Apart from the first workshop in Antsirabe, and one in the capital Antananarivo, all of the succeeding ones I attended up until 2018 were held in Toulear, in the south-western corner of Madagascar. For these our consultant accommodation was in the Norwegian Lutheran Mission House with its substantial wooden beams and planks, one of the oldest buildings in town. It was situated beside the Protestant *Katedraly*.

Workshop sessions took place in various venues in and around town – perhaps in an hotel, an empty school, or a retreat centre. Heather accompanied me for one of these workshops in Toulear, but for the most part she was in Ireland during my trips, and we corresponded by email.

A Saturday in October, 2008

Dear Heather,

The electricity is a bit ropey here in Toulear just now, and can be off for hours at a time depending on how many people are using it, so the workshop promises to have its high and low points! I believe Saturday afternoon is a particularly bad time to try to do anything requiring electricity, as folks are all busy ironing their Sunday best for the next day, and the power goes off regularly. You might say there is a lack of power for a good reason. I say it just proves what I always suspected about the value of ironing! However I hasten to add that I am very grateful for the nicely ironed T-shirts and shirts you slipped into my suitcase: thank you!

Do you remember that we were funding some of the Tanosy team to get new teeth (old ones rotted by sugar-cane consumption)? Well, the men haven't arrived from Fort Dauphin yet, but I've seen "before and after" pictures of two team members, and they are barely recognisable. In the "after" pictures they are sporting reflective sunglasses also, and look quite the film-stars! They are delighted, and I'm sure their wives are too. They wrote us a nice thank-you letter. At least I'm pretty sure it was nice, but my Tanosy doesn't stretch yet to include molars and dentures.

Sunday now

Dear Heather,

You would be proud of me. I got up at 6 a.m. this Sunday

morning to write to you. You can tell I am so much more how a Christian man should be when out here. Actually, I was awakened at 5.30 first by a very loud buzzing sound which might have been a swarm of bees outside my window, or possibly just buzzing in the ears (?!), and then by the clanging of the cathedral bell. The cathedral is just beside us here in the Mission house, and bells have been calling the faithful every half hour since. The most faithful started singing then too, probably choir practice to begin with, which has now, at 6.40, grown to a full blown service. No need to go to church: church has come to us! At one stage, the imam in the nearby mosque decided to set up a rival call to prayer – now that combination was hard to listen to! One at a time please.

The Malagasy sing many tunes which are familiar to us, tunes which the missionaries no doubt taught them, but which fit with their language and way of singing. The only difference is that they sing certain tunes without the sharps and flats we would use, so you have to watch out for that at certain points. Here are some of the ones I recognised and sang along with, in English, from the comfort of my bed:

- Work for the night is coming (an exhortation to get out of bed?)
- Bringing in the sheaves
- Follow, follow, we will follow Jesus
- Do not pass me by (no chance – they were right next door)
- Praise God from whom all blessings flow
- The bride eyes not her garment (couldn't remember first verse, so had to sing some of the verses twice...)

I was encouraged to get up and start to write, as the power was on. However, it has since gone off, so I have only about 10 minutes of battery left... zzzzz.

Sorry, computer went to sleep at that point this morning, and electricity has only just returned - at 3 p.m.! Who knows how long we will have it, so I'll send this off now while the going's good, and start another letter to you to send later.

By the way, the mystery of the buzzing was solved at breakfast. Bjorn, the Norwegian missionary, said it must have been the hundreds of bats not in my belfry, but in the real one next door, disturbed by the bell-ringers doing their Sunday morning job.

Incidentally, while we are on funny unusual things, we hear of an ethnic group - I will have to find out their name - where the women are called "les chatouilleuses", the "ticklers".

Apparently, if they don't agree with decisions or directions their male-folk are taking, they start to tickle them, and don't let up until the men change their minds. Getting their point across in an unusual way. Now I wouldn't mind if you tried that on me, but I doubt whether it would catch on in Moira Baptist church?

Will send this off now while I can, even though it's so short.

Philip

Monday

The workshop is already in full swing, with all eight translation teams present with their consultants. Today in our wee group, we spent forty-five minutes on "He who has ears to hear, let him hear." Was Jesus addressing the whole crowd, or just his disciples (and a few others whose understanding was opened)? It's important in these languages to know who is included and who is excluded. When the disciples exclaimed: "Master, we'll all be drowned!" were they including Jesus in their fearful thinking? The Tanosy need to know, to choose the correct rendering for pronoun and verb.

And then we spent about two hours trying to get a good solution for the part in the Gadarene demoniac account where the action is out of chronological sequence (The part which says: "...For Jesus had commanded/ was commanding the evil spirit to come out of the man"). Here, just adding a wee word meaning "already" seemed to satisfy the time sequence, and do the trick for Tanosy.

As we've seen before, they have only one main word for travel/ move/ walk/ drive/ sail/ ride, so there was no special verb to translate "sail" (across Galilee). Seems a pity really to reduce it to one verb, but here we are obliged to, and seem to have no option.

Lighter moments

When one of my team nods off in the heat, it's become a habit that one of the others points it out or gives me a nudge and I whip out my camera for a candid photo of the sleeping beauty. Then when he wakes up, we show him a photo of himself in repose. It's very funny, for this morning the sleeper didn't recognise himself until the other translators pointed out the colour of his T-shirt, showed the other language group at the table behind him, and so on. Then he believed them.

All good fun, and all was forgiven. He had just arrived after a long hard journey by bush-taxi after all.

Back for more in August 2012

Dear Heather,

While you were sleeping ... I was looking at my alarm clock in disbelief, and stumbling out of bed in Tana, thankful that I had shaved last night, and so didn't have to think about that in my half sleep at 4 am.

Quick shower, final shove of belongings into suitcase once again, tiptoe along the corridor to make sure colleague Ron was awake, then out into the cold foyer of the Raphia hotel. That's where you stayed when you were here, remember? There are no carpets as you know, so every little sound reverberates and threatens to wake the whole hotel up.

It is hard for me to face the world without coffee, but easier in Africa and Madagascar somehow. We didn't know if our plane was on time, or delayed for two hours as per usual, but we had to be at the airport just in case. It turned out it was on time, and left only ten minutes late, at 7.40 am.

There was the usual variety of passengers waiting: a crowd of Chinese miners, several families where parents were of mixed race, usually European/Malagasy, some loud American tourists, some quiet intellectual types probably off to look for rare orchids or shy animals, and us. We were probably not so easy to classify.

On Sunday night when we arrived at Tana airport, we got talking to a quiet American man with Malagasy wife and lovely kids, while waiting for our luggage. Turned out his name was Steve Goodman, a biologist who has contributed to thick books on Malagasy wildlife. Nice guy, would make an interesting table companion. He has a lemur named after him, the mouse lemur, known as the Goodman lemur, or lemura lehitsara (literally good-man lemur!) That's like us discovering a grammatical particle and having it named after us: like suffixus Saunderasinus. Ah well, one can but dream!

The hour-long flight down to the south of the island was lovely. You remember that journey, don't you? The sun was coming up, I had a window seat looking East, it was mostly clear, so the mountains and valleys showed up in sharp relief. It was not long before the spread-out villages and hamlets around Tana petered out, and nature took over. Mist lay in some valleys, and occasional rivers wound their way down them.

There were craters, old volcanoes, with vegetation and trees growing up the sides, little sign of humanity for miles and miles. Perhaps forty minutes of similar terrain, then we began our descent. The ground was light brown now, the hills flatter, rounder, drier. There is that point, coming down through the cloud, where the approach is really low, you feel you are almost touching the hilltop for several minutes, and wish the pilot would take her up a few hundred feet. Then the earth falls away again beneath you, and you are curving down in to land in Toulear.

Here it was pleasantly warm, with a breeze. Only a few got off along with us, others stayed on to seek pleasure, dig mines and hunt for orchids round the coast in Fort Dauphin. The arrivals hall is funny: it seems like they are playing airports. A wee luggage vehicle, two handlers, a tiny conveyor belt: they might as well just have handed us our cases as we walked across the tarmac. But it was great to see Leoni's familiar face, after four flights from Belfast City, including the eleven-hour flight from Paris. I felt grateful for the prayers of folk for this trip, especially after putting my back out a week ago tonight. It has greatly eased now, so I can look forward to the workshop without causing others inconvenience through being incapacitated.

The real work starts in earnest tomorrow. Will we be able to complete the checking of Luke's Gospel this time out?

Much love,

Philip

Tulear: approaching the end of the Luke project

Dear Heather,

Checking is going well today: some of the team are busy discussing Luke 20:37 animatedly, so I can write you a quick line. It's 3.15 pm and super hot, Kalery is trying hard to stay awake, but the Pastor is on form now and very alert. Harthmann is in town getting medicine for a stomach complaint. It's rare to have all members here at any point.

For Luke 20:30 they only needed two words in Tanosy! In many English versions, it reads: "So the second brother married the widow, but he also died." In Tanosy all they need to say is: "The second likewise." They can be concise at times. On the other hand, many words are extremely long, with fifteen letters and even more very common: Luke 21:15 contains this one for example – *fahavalondrareo* meaning *"those opposing you; your enemies"*! Different, eh?

(Later that day at 9 pm...)

Hi Heather,

A final note from me at the end of another long but satisfying day.

Ron and I have just hoovered our computer keyboards, to try to remove some of the intrusive dust we are experiencing during this weather. The earth is dry, hard and dusty too: it hasn't rained in Toulear for three to four months!

It can apparently be six months between rains in dry season here. Now we are about to shut up our laptops for the night, having both inserted a number of corrections in texts we are helping our teams with today. I was putting final changes into Luke 20, so we are ready to go on chapter 21 tomorrow.

Somehow, needed strength is granted us even during the heat of the middle of the day, though each day regularly has some low point. When this happens, I excuse myself, and get up for a short walk around the compound. Thankfully the Tanosy men are very understanding about this need, as they do the same themselves!

It is most enjoyable, during the day, to take a ten minute break occasionally, and watch the turquoise and brown bee-eaters swooping from line to tree and back to their line; or to walk along the shady avenue that curves around the concession's perimeter. The trees are nimes, firs and eucalyptus, and it's always a cool place to stroll to clear the mind, and return to the translation desk refreshed.

I have to say the food provided is very much to our taste as foreigners - plenty of vegetables, such as cabbage, carrots or manioc leaves, and the accompanying meat or chicken is great. I don't eat too much, but what I take I enjoy. It is the same with those evening meals we have out in town: tonight I had a fish kebab again, with steamed vegetables. I've avoided taking the zébu (ox) or red meat as much as possible and feel the better for it.

So now we are on the homeward stretch in Luke. I am trying to relax, and not worry about not finishing the check of the whole book, though it is still possible that we may, even before the end of this workshop.

Sorry I have to stop writing so quickly again, but little and often is the best I can do, apart from at week-ends. Hope you get a good sleep tonight. I am sleeping deeply here, for which I am grateful.

Philip

Fun with mobile phones

Pastor Mosa slowly raised his head, and looked at me directly over the translation table. A smile played on his lips, and a sparkle came to his eyes.

"Ah, Monsieur Philippe, ça doit être toi!"
I smiled in return. "Oui, c'est bien moi!"

He saw that the text message was from his consultant sitting opposite. I will play my little games, and if given any encouragement – which the Tanosy are quick to provide – the fun can sometimes come thick and fast.

Some background explanation is needed. Mobile phones had swamped Madagascar. After centuries of painfully slow communication, almost everyone now had a cheap means of staying in contact with everybody else on the island potentially, and for a relational society, this was heaven on earth.

So for our translation checking sessions, it was necessary to introduce some boundaries! Pastor Mosa had an important and responsible job as synod president, and at times had an array of at least three mobile phones in front of him, one of which would be urgently flashing at any given moment. So this meant that one of our main translators could be urgently called away from the translation table at a second's notice. The other team members all had their own little devices too, so with a little nudging from the consultant, we had to reach a compromise.

The phones would be on silent, and none of us would be permitted to consult them during sessions, only during our tea-breaks. If a phone rang, or if a phone was sneakily consulted, the miscreant would have to pay a small fine into a box placed centrally on the table.

And so, rather sneakily myself, that morning I had texted the pastor from under the table without looking down – a trick I had learned from my teenage daughters – and for his part he had been unable to resist the temptation, and had consulted his flashing phone.

We had a laugh, no-one had to pay a fine this time, and the point was well and truly taken.

Eugene

Dear Heather,

I must tell you about Eugene, our main taxi driver here in Toulear.

Eugene transports Ron and me the three miles to our workshop centre each day for 8 am, and collects us at noon again. We have siesta, and there he is, patiently waiting for us at 2.15 to take us back for the afternoon session. Without fail.

Eugene's taxi is his pride and joy, and an extension of his personality. Or maybe how he would like to be known. It is a bright red Peugeot 104, lovingly cared for and polished daily. I am glad he does not know, and is unlikely to ever see, the state of the car I drive! White sand clings to the feet of every passenger that enters his vehicle here in Toulear, but by the time he picks us up, there isn't a trace of it inside his car. I feel I should take my shoes off before getting in.

Nor could you hope to meet a more pleasant person. Thirty perhaps, open-faced, from the Vezo people group up the coast. They live from fishing, their houses often perched on stilts, but Eugene tells me he did not grow up there, cannot swim, and fears the sea. He is a townie through and through.

He is obviously a very clever person too, as he agrees with practically everything I say. I'm not sure whether I have been especially endowed with wisdom for this trip, or if he doesn't understand my accent and figures it pays to be positive. I mean, when the customer is always right, it tends to increase your clientele, doesn't it? In terms of cross-cultural ability, most folk here would put our Western international diplomats to shame.

Anyway, I like Eugene's driving. He is careful, and knows his Peugeot's limitations. Acceleration wouldn't be its strong point. So on the rare occasions he does overtake, he moves backwards and forwards in his seat, urging his steed to greater efforts, as it were.

He is not perfect, however. I have noticed an aversion to jay-walkers. He can somehow tell the difference between the many innocent bodies in his path, and the guilty, provocative ones. Pity help a defiant young man sauntering out into the roadway! Eugene will go as close to him as he dares without actually knocking him down. His expression does not change: it reminds me of certain dodgem-drivers I knew growing up.

There is a slogan written across the top of his windscreen: *Je lis la Bible, parole de Dieu*: "I read the Bible, the Word of God." At such moments of near collision, I sink down in my seat, make myself as small as possible, and pray that the cheeky young men are also illiterate.

Am attaching a picture for you of Eugene with his pride and joy.

Much love,

Philip

Lemurs and dry bones

On my way home to Ireland from Toulear, I would regularly fly up the island to Tana first, then stay overnight before taking the long-haul flight back to Paris. From there, I waited for the "Disneyland" flight back to Belfast. The latter was full of tired but excited children wearing Mickey Mouse masks, who had just happily spent all their parents' hard earned cash. Mostly by this stage of my trips, I was just itching to get back home as soon as possible, with the satisfied feeling of Mission Accomplished.

This time, though, I had planned to spend a couple of nights in Tana in more relaxed mode. Heather's niece, Pammy Best, was due to arrive as I was leaving. She was about to begin a few months working on the accounts of the Luke Project in Toulear, a most valuable contribution. As our paths were crossing, I hoped to accompany her to see some sights in Tana.

It was not a city I knew well, as I was usually simply passing through. But I knew some nice souvenir places, and had the mobile number of a reliable taxi man with a Renault R4 who could take us wherever we wanted.

"I'd like to see some lemurs!" said Pammy. "Haven't you been to Belfast zoo?" I teased. "Well yes, but it's not the same!" she protested.

So off we bounced in our friendly taxi. Tana is perched on several hills. It took an hour to cross town to the Lemur Park, up and down winding narrow streets, some cobbled, all packed with Malagasy folk in broad-brimmed hats or caps to protect them from the merciless sun.

And lemurs we saw aplenty that day. Many different types: ring-tailed, brown, ruffed and bamboo lemurs, sifakas... we learned that there are 105 recognized species and subspecies of lemur found only in Madagascar! In the Lemur Park, they weren't kept in cages, but came voluntarily to the sides of the circuit we walked around, to observe us it seemed as much as we were observing them! Some were shy, and our guide had to point out their hiding places to us. Many were cheeky though, and we had to keep track of these ones, and hang on to our belongings carefully. It was a pleasant and stimulating walk. Beside the path a number of exotic plants flourished, and my eye also caught glimpses of several birds I did not recognise.

It had been a tranquil, visually absorbing visit, which Pammy and I both thoroughly enjoyed.

"The crowds seem to be growing. Are they?" Pammy asked from the back seat of the Renault.

They were indeed, and at that point we were making painfully slow progress on the way back across town to our hotel. We slid the old car windows back for some air, and it was growing noisier by the minute. I hoped we had not stumbled into a riot of some kind. I was supposed to be a responsible adult; what could I say to Pammy's parents in my defence?

It turned out that we had stumbled across a Famadihana parade. I looked it up when Pammy and I got back to the guest house. In French, the *Le relèvement des os*, in English the *Turning of the bones*. It seemed, rather gruesomely, that the ceremony involved exhuming the dead from their graves in family crypts, wrapping them in fresh cloth, before dancing the corpses around the tombs and then replacing them. The ancestor's name will be re-written on the silk shroud, so that they will continue to be remembered.

The custom is based upon a belief that the spirits of the dead finally join the world of their ancestors only after the body's complete decomposition, and after appropriate ceremonies like the one we had encountered. Apparently, in Madagascar this became a regular ritual usually once every seven years.

Some Malagasy find positivity in the reunion of family members involved, and strengthening of family ties. Also, respect for the dead is important to them. The ceremony is controversial, in that there are health concerns for obvious reasons, and it does seem to be gradually dying out.

Personally, I felt sad. So often there was a strong sense of hopelessness and despair associated with such animistic practices. I had felt it in Ivory Coast. And at the same time, I was so glad to know and believe in the Christian message of hope in the resurrection of Jesus Christ, and the subsequent promise of the raising to eternal life of His followers.

This had been a day of such sharp contrasts for Pammy and me, what with saying hello to lemurs in the beauty of their natural habitat, and then getting caught up in the swirl of a cultural phenomenon in town.

Yet such unpredictability was what I loved about this rambling life.

Fort Dauphin

It was now September, 2018.

I crane my neck to see out the window of the aircraft. These windows and seats were definitely designed for the smaller man.

I count back. This is my sixth flight of the current trip, so only four to go after this one. All the others were in jets, this one is a turbo-prop, and the landscape of Madagascar can be clearly seen at this height below the whirring propellers.

To be honest, plane travel has become a bit wearisome. In and out of airports, lengthy security queues. However, I am enjoying this flight, for we are flying from Antananarivo to Fort Dauphin, where I am due to work with the Tanosy team in their language location for the first time. On many previous trips, both the team and myself were displaced, travelling either to Antsirabe, Tana or Toulear for joint workshops with the other language teams.

This time, for two weeks, I am in Fort Dauphin, on the south-eastern tip of the island. Next stop Antarctica, though I have no intention of abandoning the heat.

I am in First Class, I think because there were no available economy class tickets left when my colleagues arranged the flight for me. I smiled as I checked in my baggage, and made a mental note to send a picture of the labels to my sister later. *VIP -Première Classe*: I like it. Actually, though, in the end I was treated little differently from the other passengers. The only distinction was that a small curtain was swished across for a bit of privacy for the chosen few.

After a while we left the central uplands, and flew down the eastern coast of the island, with mile after mile of straight white strand and the Indian ocean below on my left. Then it was inland a little towards another range of mountains. Now the plane was starting to make its approach into Fort Dauphin, and anticipatory music began to play softly and pleasantly. We traversed a small lagoon, overflew some farmers busy on their land, and then all of a sudden we were down, bumping along the airfield towards what seemed a tiny terminal.

It always warms the heart when you see your name on one of those signboards the welcoming committees hold aloft to arriving passengers. There it was, though the writer had misjudged the length of my name, so the final –s had got disconnected from the Saunder. Fine on a signboard, but not great on a tombstone, I thought. I was reminded of the true story a friend told me: "Lord she was thin" proclaimed the epitaph! The vital, missing "-e" could be found on the next line.

Anyway, Saunder was close enough, my man spots me, gives a thumbs up, and I turn to await my luggage. Before long, out I go into the rather humid heat. He protects me from some "helpers", but the general atmosphere is friendly rather than aggressive.

"Kaleta hotel, m'sieur?" "Merci!"And we set off in his double cabin four by four. I try out some of my Tanosy greetings on him, and he is all pleased, and I am all pleased he understands me. Feelings of pleasure all round then.

I am aware that this is a remote place, and yet... there is a familiarity about it. This is not so very different, is it, from the experience of the wee lad in Singapore almost sixty years earlier? The one who ran barefoot down to the *kampong* to sit at a table with his friend and learn Malay? God really does know what He is doing in our lives. And here and now, looking out the passenger window of the four by four, the sense of familiarity came from a mixture of knowing the Tanosy men in my team who I would soon be meeting, of recognising the fruit and vegetables on the stalls, inhaling the smell of the fish market, and watching an undisturbed world of people going about their daily business. I know I will enjoy being here.

The Kaleta Hotel is faded French grandeur. It stands tall in a prime position overlooking the old customs port and harbour, feeling cool inside with its high ceilings. The guests are spaced out under the covered atrium, most at computers or smart-phones using the hotel's free Wi-Fi.

The young man at reception is most helpful. He is clearly keen to practise his English with this Irishman, leading me up a grand wide flight of wooden stairs, along an open passage-way to my room which has, he explains, a view of the sea. He has trouble getting the TV to work, but I tell him it doesn't matter, I don't watch TV much. I prefer to sleep now, after my long journey. We agree to meet up later, so that he can further practise his English. Soon, after telling me the time for breakfast, he retreats discreetly.

I cross to the window, pull back a net curtain, and open the shutter. This was truly a wow moment! I catch my breath. It is not just the strong breeze that takes my breath away. The stunning view I am to have for the next two weeks is the picture on the front of this book!

A happy reunion

It is morning. I have already eaten some of the oats I always carry on trips, so am ready for whatever bonus the hotel breakfast provides. It is a *croissant,* a *pain raisin* from the *pâtisserie*, some banana and papaya – all of which are fine by me. The coffee is very satisfactory too.

I step out the front door of the hotel with a nod to the doorman. The strong easterly breeze seems to be a constant here. You can understand how cyclones can be so dangerous during their season. I lean into the wind as I leave, and am glad of the shelter of the churchyard when I reach it. The church, rising to my left as I cross the thoroughfare, is imposing and impressive.

Pastor Mosa is waiting with a broad smile of welcome. After a warm embrace, he unlocks a gate, and we make our way towards his house where the translation checking is to take place. With a gesture towards the church, he explains that he is about to retire now from his life's ministry, and wants to concentrate on the Tanosy Bible translation more from now on. As we walk and talk, a line of ducks precedes us, waddling along without a care in the world it seems. And yet they have every reason to be fearful, as *ganagana* is a favourite dish here. I often eat it given the choice, so I take care not to form any emotional relationship with a duck while I am in Madagascar.

We make our way slowly up an incline, propelled by the wind however, which is now at our backs. You do not rush life here. We come to his house, which is made of sturdy wooden planks and a tin roof. It has a very pleasant shape and design, but is clearly quite old now. We move down some more wide steps, ducking underneath a traveller's palm, and on to a wooden balcony with several boards which shift under our feet.

Pastor Mosa opens a creaking door, and half a dozen smiling faces greet us. Then it is back to exchange of greetings. They test my memory of Tanosy phrases:

Good morning, Philip!
Good morning, Elersen!
How are you doing? Are you well?
Very well. And you?
Doing well. What's new?
No, nothing new, nothing bad. Not one single thing!

They are pleased that I remember the last phrase – *dre raiky* - as they tell me it is truly Tanosy in the context, but I must remember to add the correct dismissive hand gesture to accompany it!

Madame Pasteur is already busy with cups and plates for morning break, so I am in for a further breakfast it seems. The team has been there since early morning, preparing, so they are ready for some nourishment. I'd best go easy this time...

There is much joy in meeting up again, especially since it is finally in their own language area. The event is tinged with sadness, though, as one of the team members – Davida – has been unwell, and is recovering slowly in town after a stroke. We will visit him soon as a team, and bring a gift to help with his medical expenses.

A younger lady in her forties has joined the team in his place, so around the table that first morning were Fideline, along with regulars Elersen, Philippe Meeti, Harthmann, Mosa and myself. They are excited to show me the Tanosy Gospel of Luke which has been published since I was last in Madagascar. It is an attractive book, with a good size of font for new readers, and my heart is warmed as I look through it, all too keenly aware of the hard work it represents that we had all put in as a team. The Tanosy can now read the Gospel story for themselves, praise God!

After tea-break, we settle into work.

The checking session

As a translation consultant, one of the questions I am most asked is this:

"If you aren't a fluent speaker of a language, how can you check it?"

While every consultant has his or her preferred method, there are certain common principles we share. All of us want to make sure that the meaning of the translation comes across clearly and accurately with respect to the Greek original, and that the language used is natural for native speakers. Stating the obvious perhaps, translation is not about simply transferring *words* from one language to another; it's about transferring *meanings* of whole sentences, phrases and words. The best translations will not seem like translations at all. So how do you manage as a consultant to verify all this, if you don't know the language well yourself?

My own preferred method is to listen very carefully as the team reads out its draft translation. I try to have all my antennae out, prepared to intervene on different levels, as necessary. So after a whole paragraph has been read aloud to begin with to establish the context, a single verse will be read through in Tanosy by one of the team. I watch for any hesitation or stumbling over words or phrases, which may indicate some unnaturalness, or may simply mean that a particular word needs to be broken up into further segments for ease of reading.

Then the reader retraces their steps, and reads phrase by phrase, this time with another Tanosy person giving an oral backtranslation into French for my benefit. If the backtranslator's French is limited, then it is advisable for a written backtranslation to be prepared by that person in advance of the session.

Some consultants insist on a "naïve" backtranslator being present, that is someone who has not been involved in the translation drafting itself. This has some advantages, in that such a person will not know what a passage is supposed to mean! It can however slow the process up considerably, as the naïve backtranslator searches for appropriate vocabulary in the language of wider communication (in this case, French).

The consultant needs to distinguish between genuine miscomprehension, and a simple inability at times to find the right French words to convey the text's meaning. It is not always straightforward, as the two languages – in this case Tanosy and French - rarely have word for word equivalence.

Some suggestions for improvement are simple. On a basic level, while listening to the whole verse being read, the consultant might suggest punctuation to improve the flow, or even to allow the reader to catch a breath! Dividing up a long sentence can also improve the style of the work.

The main job of the consultant, though, is to check for accuracy. The team often spots unnatural renderings itself as they read. They sense when meaning is not clear too. But a translation may be natural, it may also be clear, but it will be clearly wrong if the meaning of the original is missed! Sometimes it is just a little word missing, and the most common one is "all". It is rather important when that little missing word is "not" – as famously occurred in one translation's version of the Ten Commandments!

More often, however, a word is "nearly right" and a better one can and needs to be found. In Malagasy draft translations, we found this to be a common failing: more rigour needed to be exercised by the teams to find the *mot juste*, and not to be content with a generic substitute.

So a passage such as Galatians 5: 19-23 will require a lot of close attention, to make sure the terms are distinguished from one another, and not summarised as "bad and evil things" or merged together as "good, godly qualities":

[19] "Now the works of the flesh are plain: fornication, impurity, licentiousness,
[20] idolatry, sorcery, enmity, strife, jealousy, anger, selfishness, dissension, party spirit,
[21] envy, drunkenness, carousing, and the like. I warn you, as I warned you before, that those who do such things shall not inherit the kingdom of God.
[22] But the fruit of the Spirit is love, joy, peace, patience, kindness, goodness, faithfulness,
[23] gentleness, self-control; against such there is no law.

It must be admitted that this is no small task, in any language! What is the difference between 'jealousy' and 'envy', for instance? Moreover, important regularly occurring terms in the Biblical text (Key terms) should where possible be translated consistently in the new translation, and spellings must certainly be consistent. Thankfully, we have great computer programmes to help us out with this aspect of the translation task nowadays.

In practice, for those two weeks, as I heard the team read the Tanosy translation of parts of the Acts and sections of Genesis, I was listening for underlying meaning rather than surface form. The order of words in their Tanosy sentences was different, so usually I had to carry the action in my head, and only at the end of the sentence find out who was doing it – when the backtranslator would exclaim a triumphant "...Paul!" for my benefit. It is nice when you know a team well, and they can sympathise with their consultant in his trials! I appreciated that, as I enjoyed the sense of humour with which the Tanosy team go about this serious and vital business of translating the Holy Scriptures.

Back to the translation table in Fort Dauphin. Now the first morning session is over in Pastor Mosa's house, our heads are spinning with the required concentration over several hours, and it is time to come apart and rest a while.

We have agreed that I will eat most of my meals at the hotel, to lessen the pressure on the Mosa household, so at lunch-time I pack my laptop bag, open the creaking door and cross back over the loose boards, noticing a very large yellow and black spider on his web about the height of my head under the traveller's palm. I make my way back to the Kaleta under a sun that is by now high and burning the skin of my neck.

I negotiate the yellow tuktuks - small motorised three-wheeler vehicles for hire in town – and reach the sanctuary of the cool hotel. Then it is up the wooden stairs to my room for siesta, leaving the window open for a welcome breeze from the sea far below.

Relaxation

"How do you switch off from this concentrated checking?" – is another question we are often asked.

For starters, Heather and I always have a book on the go, and that book will not be a technical one. A light novel or biography helps us transition from checking to sleep, and more often than not, even a couple of pages does the trick.

In Madagascar, it is not hard to relax. I bring a good camera, and have fun photographing the wildlife around me. There are the game parks with all sorts of lemurs, but a simple walk anywhere is enough to reveal an exotic bird or insect. One day I marvel at a huge mother-of-pearl butterfly, with wings like parachutes. A few days later, on that same traveller's palm where the spider lived, I see a lizard painted in incredible pastel colours, as if a four-year-old child had been having fun with a paint-box.

Hunters and gatherers

But this time out, in Fort Dauphin, it is the fisherfolk who capture my attention. From my hotel room, through my telephoto lens, I can admire their various methods and their courage, as they venture out into quite rough seas in the bay.

The men leave harbour in bigger dug-out boats, and their craft can be seen in the distance bobbing about in the waves. They are hunting for the bigger fish. But fishing starts early in life for the Malagasy youngsters. Daily, unless the sea is especially turbulent, I see a group of six or eight boys and girls move out from the brilliant white sand into the sparkling sea, carrying between them a net stretched out horizontally. It looks like a large mosquito net, and soon their feet cannot touch the seabed, and they are swimming round in a wide semi-circle, attempting to trap some fish. They drag this net back ashore, and up the beach, picking small fish out from among the pile of seaweed and flotsam.

The fish go into a bucket, and out the group goes again, joined this time by their mother, who looks heavily pregnant. It is a tough life, and this is not play for the children. For many of them, their livelihood is at stake. They repeat this exhausting process a number of times, then when the sun comes up, they rest in some shade by the shore, mending their nets. At the end of the day, as the sun goes down, I see a dozen folk, standing in a tight group under a palm tree, with remarkable patience and good nature dividing out the spoils of the day's fishing. They can't have caught much: but what they have they share admirably.

As I look on, I recall that such were called by the Lord Jesus to follow Him, as He walked by the shores of Galilee, though the disciples were considerably older than these young ones.

Hard work and rest. This is how it was with the translation checking too. There are certainly setbacks, and Davida has not been able to return to the team for several months now. But there are encouragements too. Three of the hotel staff ask me for copies of Tanosy Luke, and looking back over my shoulder, I see the receptionist reading his copy of the Gospel with a smile and clear interest.

This makes it all worthwhile. Slowly but surely, Bible translation is having an impact and making a difference.

As I travel between countries and workshops, my hair doesn't stop growing. So to achieve a modicum of respectability, I need at times to visit hairdressers on foreign soil, far from the comfort zone of Sporty's barbershop in Heather's hometown of Lurgan, my usual choice. I am a reluctant recruit, it has to be said.

The Jordanian barber's in Jo'burg

He seemed such a nice young man. You know, soft smile, welcoming, gently wrapping the towel round my shoulders and neck... courteous to a fault.

"This is not a hairdresser's, this is a *real* barber's," my friend Rob had explained, in order to prepare me. At first sight, I was not convinced I should be there. There were too many long knives and scalpels around for my liking. Word associations flooded my mind – barber, barb, barbarous, barbarian – but I quickly pushed these back and concentrated on the present. I was there to get my hair cut, and it certainly needed it.

"Coffee?" my new barber friend inquired. "Yes, please" I answered. Something familiar, and pleasant. A lady soon arrived with a fancy silver ornament presumably containing a cup of coffee. "The real Arabian sort," enthused my man in a whisper.

By this time, he was ready, and got down to the job at hand. What happened in the next half hour is a bit of a blur, to be honest. It was a maelstrom of sensation.

I had asked for a thinning out of the main part, with the hair to just fall on top of my ears. Keep the length at the back, please. A number two on the beard, and a hot shave. All as at home, apart from the hot shave, but Rob had said this was an absolute 'must' and that I shouldn't shave that morning, so I hadn't.

My new Jordanian friend set to work. Removing my glasses

with care, he took an electric razor, and in no time had trimmed my beard. This is great I thought. Then he started to pummel, he snipped, a pull of the hair here, and push of the head there. No hanging about. A comment or two in Arabic to his neighbour, and then the hair-trim was over. Next, he took a wad of perhaps cotton (had to guess without my glasses), dipped it into a bowl, and stuffed it up my right nostril! The left nostril quickly followed. I opened my mouth to breathe. Surely he wouldn't stuff something in my mouth too? No, he attacked the ears next. With everything plugged, I was not quite feeling myself, but I closed my eyes and remembered that my brother-in-law had once survived this treatment, so I probably would too.

What happened next was excruciating. The plugs were whipped out, one by one, along with two decades of unsuspecting hairy nose and ear growth. I am pleased to say I did not bring the house down with my screaming. Inside of me, I screamed a lot.

In torture, I believe they alternate pain with pleasure. The next part was pleasurable. Gentle Ali - not his real name, but apt I think for a Baba – anyway, Ali from Jordan spread a vanilla-scented cream over my cheeks, and those parts with stubble. Then he bent over real close with a razor, and tackled every cheek hair one by one in the safety of their follicles. The neck was next. At this point I took care not to mention that I was a Bible translator, since the TV monitors in the shop were all busy showing the Faithful bowing down towards the East.

Happily, the neck was soon finished. I was by now feeling remarkably 'clean', and it struck me that in my normal life, I must have let my grooming drift somewhat. Perhaps everyone thought I looked scruffy, and I didn't realise it?

Time for torture again. Ali started twisting some thread between his fingers it seemed, and busied himself in the ear region. Whatever he was doing, the twanging sounded like a Jewish harp – but couldn't have been of course – and the soreness as the fuzz around the outside of my ears and forehead was removed was sharp and delicate, as opposed to the deep pain of the nasal plug removal.

Is there anything left of me, I wondered?

Ali now tipped my chair forward, stood me up, and led me carefully to another seat, where I was reclined further, and my hair washed and shampooed in pleasantly warm water. Hot cloths wiped the vanilla off cheeks and neck, I was given a warm comfort blanket for everywhere, brought back to my first seat, reunited with my glasses, and asked to admire the result.

I have to admit that I looked like a new man, and that was undoubtedly necessary, though it had felt more like the dentist's than the hairdresser's. I felt guilty to be relieved it was over, and yet there is no doubt that there was a marked improvement. No gain without pain, and all that.

And Ali the barber from Jordan had seemed such a nice young man. As I got up, he held out his hand to be shaken. This was a first also for me and a barber. We parted as friends. At that point, I realised that I had probably passed my test. At no point had I screamed, or let my friend Rob down.

All was well: I gave myself a virtual pat on the back. Then Ali added helpfully: "Your son has just stepped out of the shop. He says he'll be back shortly." My son? Well, I suppose Rob could be my son – just about.

I surveyed the white locks on the floor surrounding my tormentor's chair, and reluctantly forgave him his understandable mistake.

Israel

"Why are they all shouting?" I asked.

"Because we love noise," responded our Jewish guide. "We love to shout, clap and sing!"

This was Jerusalem, and our little tour group was taking a rest in the shade, inside the old walled city. Nearby, and it seemed all around us, those ancient walls were resounding with the clamour of a *Bar mitsvah*, where the family of a young Jewish boy was conducting a coming of age ceremony. It seemed like an excuse for a joyous party, balloons and all, and to judge by the number of teenage boys milling around, all proudly sporting their broad-brimmed black hats, dark suits and white shirts, it appeared as if the popular young man was just itching to join his older pals and become an adult. And to swap his circular cap for a splendid black hat!

So much was new to me: there was just so much to assimilate. "Biblical Byways" was a study tour which lasted most of two weeks, and it was a privilege to be participants. It was intensive, and intended to be a course which took in as much as possible of the country, relating each place or site to the corresponding biblical narrative. Daily, our trust in the reliability of the biblical accounts was being strengthened by leaders Les and Cathy Bruce. We travelled from Beersheba in the south, to Dan in the far north, marvelling at the variety of landscapes and back-stories in this small country of Israel. Each night was spent in a different town and hostelry, which included Bethlehem and Nazareth.

What follows are a few personal impressions from our visit. I'll not attempt to cover the multitude of facts we tried our best to take in from day to day.

I've mentioned noise, and this was so true of Jerusalem. To me it seemed a controlled yet chaotic city where something momentous seemed about to happen at every moment. A city where the senses were bombarded with people – locals, tourists, religious figures, children – hurrying, scurrying to destinations known only to themselves. A city where perfume-laden air wafted from exotic shop-fronts, and where winding cobbled side-alleys echoed with boisterous greetings. It was no surprise that Jesus and His disciples wanted to escape to the Mount of Olives for some space to pray and reflect. In the gloom of the ancient church of the Holy Sepulchre in Jerusalem, I had a strong sense of sentimental superstition, rather than of true worship, and as I watched a pilgrim woman kneel to kiss the worn, cold stone, it made me a bit sad.

Yet all this contrasts sharply in my memory with the tranquillity of Galilee. It was on these largely unspoiled shores that my mind felt free to be transported back to Bible times, when Jesus walked and talked, taught and healed, and sailed on both calm and stormy waters. Watching Heather dance to a gentle Jewish song on board a wide wooden fishing boat on Galilee, was one of the highlights for me to remember and savour.

Another happy memory is singing in the Beit Gulbrin Bell Caves. These are man-made, and underground, hewn out of the chalk in times past, and used for all sorts of purposes: storage, cultic worship, keeping animals, shelter. It was cool down there, in every sense. Our group had a number of great harmonisers, and it was a taste of heaven to join with them in praising God, with the help of those fantastic subterranean acoustics.

It is Israel's contrasts which remain indelibly with me. The heights of Mount Carmel, where God enabled Elijah to triumph over the prophets of Baal. The depths of the Dead Sea, where we struggled to stay upright as we bathed in the salt saturated water.

Everywhere we looked, it seemed, there was parched earth, but often close to flowing water. Thirsty land, and living streams. The extreme dryness of southern Israel, the aridity of the Judean desert with its camel trains, and Bedouin tribes surviving in tents on meagre resources. The Masada hill fortress, where its Jewish inhabitants survived a Roman siege for three years, because of its underground cisterns providing life-sustaining water. We saw Jewish families on picnics, with patriarchs splashing joyously in the tumbling streams of En-Gedi, right next to the caves hewn in barren rock, where David hid from King Saul who was pursuing him.

We sat beside the muddy river Jordan on the eastern side of the country, and later the clear cool Mediterranean Sea on the western side. Caesarea on the coast, with its fresh breezes must have been a fine playground for the Romans with its amphitheatre, chariot race-course (hippodrome) and one of Herod's many palaces reaching into the sea. A thriving port it once was, but with a dark side: this was where the Apostle Paul was brought to be kept under house arrest, removed from the Jews who were hounding him. The Romans were admirable master-builders on the one hand, but harsh and cruel task-masters if you crossed them.

We visited Dan in the far north, on the borders of Lebanon and Syria. Once again, it was wonderful to witness as we travelled how the Israelis have made the desert "flower", with swathes of green cultivation springing from the desert. Date palm plantations flourishing out of nothing. Our group climbed up to a vantage point through green pastures, ferns and exotic trees, stepping back and forth across limpid, rushing streams. At the top, senses refreshed, we listened as our guide pointed across the valley to the north.

"Damascus is that way. Then you see that village over yonder to the right?" the guide continued matter-of-factly. "ISIS are there, but we are keeping an eye on them. Have a look up there to the left!" We spotted what looked like recent earth-works. "Up there, people are building tunnels into Israel."

Below us was a burnt-out armoured vehicle, a grim reminder of war-torn times. Now at least there was a peace, of sorts. We couldn't help but join with the nation in a silent prayer for peace for Israel, the kind of peace we had ourselves experienced so recently, further south on Lake Galilee.

We knew that ultimately, it was only the Man of Galilee who would bring about lasting peace.

Zambia

Tuesday, 14th July, 2015

Dear families,

This is our first morning in Zambia.

First impressions have been pretty good. We really like the climate at the moment. Even in the hottest part of the day, when we arrived, the heat was pretty tolerable. Heather is especially pleased, as she has not experienced anything other than strong heat and humidity on the African continent.

When we got off the plane and walked across the tarmac, it was warm with a light breeze. There is that sunlight which gives a slightly orange-yellow tinge to everything it hits. Officials were present here and there, but there was no aggression or nastiness. Nor did we witness rugby scrums, so common at certain airports. Four queues (for diplomats, tourists, residents and those with work permits) had started to form, and being at the front and fairly quickly off the plane, we were at about number 12 of the tourist queue. There was an air of order at that point.

In the small reception area, there were a lot of excited Chinese in uniforms, probably expecting someone important off the plane. Many photos were taken in groups. There was certainly a relaxed attitude to photos overall, unusual at airports.

It took a long time for our queue to advance, so we were glad we had got off quickly. Pity the poor folks behind us! Through the gaps behind the kiosks we could see all of the luggage arriving off the plane, ours hopefully included.

One optimistic and rather brash family marched up purposefully to the counter ahead of us, their three young girls in tow: two adult men and a woman. It seemed pretty obvious they were trying to jump the queue, using their children as a pretext. Our queue members were not amused. This was an English colony after all; you should be respectful and take your turn! Thankfully, the rather prim middle-aged woman who was ponderously handling the new tourists took the same attitude, and mostly ignored them. They were very persistent, and it would have been easy to give in. Another man on his own was trying the same tactic, trying to convince the officials that he should be taken earlier too.

Heather and I got to the counter finally, and each had our photos taken. It was a good time to be Irish, and we sensed that there was clearly a positive attitude there. Well done the early Irish in Zambia, I say!

We were waved through customs, so what is often the

hardest part of coming into an African country turned out to be really quite smooth. Slow, but smooth.

It was taxi-driver Clarence who met us with a sign board. I think our names were even spelt correctly. He drives a Toyota, just like two-thirds of all car owners in Zambia, it seems. There are Nissans, Mazdas, some BMWs, Range Rovers too, but if you want spare parts, explained Clarence, go for Toyota.

Heather dozed off on the hour-long drive to Flying Mission Zambia's concession, on the other side of Lusaka. That indicated that Clarence was a good driver! Roads were quiet and easy at first, only a few shallow potholes here and there. When we hit centre of town, and on the way out again, traffic was much heavier. We noted with pleasure the variety of trees, including flame-trees, and jacaranda in bloom. There were supermarkets and a mall or two, plus several large Casinos which the orientals apparently like and frequent. Then there were markets with very fragile looking shelters that wouldn't withstand much stormy weather, but it hadn't rained for four months according to Clarence. Hard on the farmers, we thought. Next rains not expected until November! Mostly Clarence understood our accents. When he couldn't make out what I was saying, he politely asked: "Come again...?" Better than the N Irish "Whassat ye say?"

I learned quite a few things about Clarence, his family and work, along with a few tidbits about the country and its politics.

We arrived at our destination at five o'clock. A lovely wee family is putting us up for two nights. Maryann is in her mid-thirties, Guilliamo ten years older. He is of Mennonite background, having grown up as a child in Mexico, and having spoken Plattdeutsch and Hochdeutsch in school. He is a pilot, a groundsman/gardener for the airstrip and business manager as required! He was late for supper, as a short term worker had got lost shopping in a Mall, with her phone not receiving calls. She did finally turn up.

We turned in early, and I had a good nine hours' sleep, in two installments as usual these days, with an hour of reflection in the middle! There was plenty to absorb. This cross-cultural experience is fascinating as always.

It has been a promising start.

Wednesday, 15th July, 2015

Dear families,

Heather and I have moved now to stay beside the airstrip, where Flying Mission Zambia planes take off on their errands of mercy, ferrying all sorts of people on all sorts of missions to remote parts of the country.

We moved from the family house around midday. It was hard to leave the three lively children, who, they said, viewed us as "grandpaw" and "grandmaw". Not hard emotionally – as we had only stayed there for two nights – just physically difficult to leave with all the last minute animals, pictures, treasures and tricks they wanted to show us. The wee girl gave us a goodbye card, while the wee boy gave us a bag of assorted sweets. Lovely.

Then it was down to business. Two of the other consultants –
Jim Clarke and Neil Baumgartner - have arrived from the
States now; we expect Tom Jacob to arrive from South Africa
on Friday. So the four of us had our first informal meeting out
in the open air, moving our plastic chairs around to escape the
direct sunlight from time to time. Heather and I are listening
hard, trying to come up to speed quickly about the country,
the languages, the systems, the translation teams, and what
has been achieved so far.

As Irish, we find it easy to relate to Americans. They are like
us, but more so, if you get my meaning. An American introvert
is an Irish extrovert. So Heather is pretty normal to them,
while I am like an inscrutable oriental, until they get to know
me. I don't mean to be unsociable, I'm just trying to figure
things out...

We talked programmes, they talked schedules. We asked
about supermarkets, they answered malls. They mentioned
peanut butter, we wondered about real butter. Tomorrow we
are all to go into town, to stock up on some items we can't get
upcountry, in Mongu. There is some special, long-lasting and
nutritious bread to pick up too. A SIM card for use in Zambia.
Work permit papers to submit. We are here as tourists this
time, but hope to be granted work permits by the time of our
next visit.

Money wise, staying at this guesthouse we don't have to use
cash much, but we will soon have to, so we are learning how
to divide Zambian Kwacha to get pounds. US dollars go down

well in exchange, pounds not bad, but how will they view our Bank of Ireland sterling notes? Euros are not an option except in certain banks.

This is a great place (Flying Mission Zambia) to make the transition from Western life to rural African life. One of those missionary oases with which we are so familiar, and a most pleasant one at that. Heather and I agreed earlier that it is such a good idea to come a few days early just to disengage from Ireland, and prepare for something completely different, even if we had the disappointment of missing our province's marches on the 12th of July. ☺

Westward Ho!

The long road between Lusaka and Mongu heads directly West, so you have the sun on your back the whole way. We make an early start, as the 600 kilometre trip (375 miles) takes a minimum of nine hours with stops, so we want to get as far as we can before it becomes too hot to think. Arriving before nightfall would be a bonus too.

We five consultants are jammed into the minibus with our luggage surrounding us, and though most of the seat-belts work, a roll or two of the vehicle would not cause too much damage to the passengers, as they would be unlikely to shift far, even upside down.

The road is apparently good for about two thirds of the journey, but very poor for the remainder. We have been warned that we are likely only to experience two emotions: boredom and terror. The boredom is due to the uniformly flat landscape we pass through for much of the way; the terror is from the state of certain vehicles crabbing towards you at high speed on potentially uneven surfaces.

To be warned is to be forearmed, but to be honest, our American colleagues are better prepared than we are. Perhaps it has to do with the nature of their roads in parts of the US, where they set their vehicles to Cruise Control and tell them where to go? In any case, electronic devices emerge from nowhere to keep them amused, and snacks appear from rucksacks which they readily and generously share with their Irish counterparts.

We don't traditionally "do" straight roads in Ireland, which is of course what makes it so "cute" to outsiders. We are used to being entertained by our countryside. We have coffee-shops and tea-houses, bars and watering-holes every few miles, which shows where we place our priorities. So the American cookies went down well with the Irish that day.

But I must be fair. The road West has its very attractive spots. Most welcome are the places where you could most profitably spend one or two Kwacha by the roadside. We call it "spending a penny". We were to become very familiar with these no doubt once upon a time pristine, white buildings, with "gentlemen" and "ladies" painted in faded black on their sides. An owner or his relative would appear out of the bush or the village to collect our fees, and a plastic cylinder was available, fitted with a tap and filled with water for ablutions should you want to risk it!

The trick, I gathered, was to time your arrival at these conveniences *not* to coincide with the Shalom express bus also bound for Mongu, all of whose occupants had the same idea as yourself.

There was one of these establishments right on the edge of the Kafue Gamepark, adjacent to stalls selling fruit and vegetables. So we set off again on that first trip, relieved and armed with a bunch of lady-finger bananas, to see what adventures lay next.

On that trip, and all subsequent trips, the ninety minutes spent traversing this open Game reserve, part of which the Mongu road passes through, are without doubt the highlight of the day. It is an enormous park: at 8,600 square miles about the size of Wales. You never know what you might see: common are deer of all kinds and shapes - from elegant gazelle to muscular waterbuck. The monkeys and baboons are not shy, and warthogs splash through muddy water-holes. You might catch sight of a zebra, a monitor lizard, a mongoose, hyenas or a group of majestic elephants. We have had good views of buffalo and hippos. There are big cats too, including lions, but to see these you have to leave very early in the morning, and we are usually more concerned with catching up on sleep after our long flights from Europe and America. But we live in hope of spotting a lion one day.

In the Gamepark, my love of birds is satisfied too, and I keep on the alert for unusual sightings. Eagles, falcons, vultures, herons and egrets, saddleback cranes, the emerald flashes of green starlings, the turquoise of bee-eaters and kingfishers: I'd love to stop and stare, but there is no time. We must move on.

We have one or two favourite pit-stops. Towards the end of the Gamepark lies Mukambi Lodge, a beautifully constructed collection of thatched buildings on the edge of the broad Kafue river, which we rarely pass without dropping in for a coffee or an icy Coke for a pleasant half hour. From its high vantage-point, we can enjoy the fresh breeze from the river below, listen to the weaver-birds chirping in the palms, scan the water for the hippos they say are plentiful, and fortify ourselves for the next stage of our trip, to start with over some very poor roads.

Then there is a garage with some shops beside it in the sizeable town of Kaoma, with meat-pies and a bathroom facility, and this oasis provides a welcome break for tummy muscles stretched and strained by the worst section of road. Once we leave Kaoma, we know we are on the last lap, with about two hours to go.

"Don't the Kwangwa live around here?" I ask our driver. "Yes, they do," he responds, with a sweep of his arm to his left. He points to the south, down a white, sandy track. "Any of these roads now will take you to their villages. But it's a long way down. If you're fortunate, you catch a vehicle going that way. Otherwise, you must go by ox-cart, or bicycle, or you walk."

I peer between the trees and scrub into the distance as we travel along. The Kwangwa translation team is the one I am to work with in Mongu. The terrain seems inhospitable and not very fertile to my untrained eye. There are clusters of huts forming small villages, with occasional patches of green where vegetables are grown. On the roadside, we pass tall hessian bags full of charcoal, obviously for sale. Families busy themselves tilling the soil, hauling the bags, loading produce on to bicycles or oxcarts.

There is a rhythm to their lives, which finds echoes in villages all over Africa. The men go out to work in their plantations, and build or repair their village huts in between. The women look after their little ones, and prepare the family food. To rest, the women sit on benches in the shade and braid each other's hair as they chat; the men play chequers in the shade of a mango tree.

"These people have very little," I mused, "but they are courageous. To eke out an existence with such meagre resources..." That day I admired the industry of the local people, and I have admired them increasingly ever since, as I have got to know them.

Yet however we try to balance out and manage the journey from Lusaka, the road is long and arduous, and the day is inevitably tiring, so it is a relief to reach the outskirts of Mongu, and know that we are nearly at Mutoya Camp. Small businesses and churches vie for space at the roadside. We smile at the signboards: *"God's Time is Best Investments"; "Patience Trading"; "Holy Corner Investment Company"; "All Smiles Beauty Parlour".*

Leaving the centre of Mongu town, we head southwards. If we kept going along this road, I reckoned, we'd hit Livingstone and the Victoria Falls in a day or so. But soon, after travelling for about a mile along a ridge high above the Zambesi flood-plain, we find ourselves bumping down a rutted sandy track, through two sets of gates, and into the campsite on a hillside, which was to be our home for the next three weeks.

It seemed like a garden of Eden after the heat and dust of the day.

A date in Mongu

After two weeks of workshop, and intensive involvement with twenty or so people, all in each other's pockets, it was time for Heather and me to have a quiet, intimate date together. In Mongu, the options for this are limited, we soon discovered. I mean it is a fine town, there are no bandits, no packs of rabid dogs, no heavy traffic clogging the thoroughfares. Trouble is, there is not a lot of anything, when it comes to choosing a special spot for a date.

The lady wanted to try to buy a long skirt or a dress, so the first part of our date was to look for the *Pep* store, a popular "Going Concern" which imports clothes from South Africa. My role was to tag along behind, holding the massive blue plastic basket provided, in case we spotted a bargain.

Our first taxi ride together in Zambia had been well negotiated, we had not paid over the odds, and when we crossed the drain in front of the shop, we had chosen the widest of the six little bridges and didn't fall in. Date going great so far.

The shop was full of items hard to find in this corner of Zambia. So half an hour later, we arrived at the checkout with a new pillow for Heather, a plastic thermos with two cups, and a long pink patterned skirt Heather was a little doubtful about, but which might "do".

We queued up to pay. About 160 Kwacha in total: 13 pounds or so. I believe this spending spree entitled us to what happened next.

Heather, standing behind me, was asked would she like to pick a balloon. The girl pointed up at the shop ceiling. There were about ten balloons to choose from. Heather looked nonplussed, no doubt thinking of her image as a mature, middle-aged white woman, if she were to take her trophy along the street with her. Thinking quickly, she said to me: "I can always give it to that wee girl behind us in the queue!" The assistant called a tall Zambian assistant over to help Heather in her choice of balloon.

The first one they inspected seemed to Heather to have a fly in it, revealed by the shop light behind. She moved to the next one. It seemed to be the same, so she just pointed at one of them, whereupon the tall man plucked the balloon, burst it, and grabbed a piece of paper as it fluttered down. He unfurled a little note, which read: "Two coffee cups." And this was our prize, it turned out, after taking our note to the customer services desk. The lady behind us was not so fortunate: she won a blue plastic brush and dustpan, which it seemed she had won several times before. We felt sorry for her, but we weren't for changing, as we also would have little use for the dustpan set, whereas the coffee cups might always come in handy. Anyone who knows me will testify to that.

It somehow seemed appropriate that one of the china cups (from China actually!) had an owl on it, and the other proclaimed boldly: "Hello Sunshine!" I'll leave you to guess who owns which cup now.

Heather felt our date had started well. I calculated we had received a ten per cent discount. So we both left *Pep* with a spring in our step.

The Kuomboka – a Barotseland tradition

I mentioned previously that my personal preference was to avoid big tourist attractions, and instead to try to discover what a country is like underneath the razzmatazz.

The *Kuomboka* ceremony is an exception, though. It is an extravagant pageant worth attending, evidenced by the fact that many Zambians themselves like to watch it.

However, it does not always occur every year, a date cannot be put definitively in the diary, and here is why. The *Kuomboka* marks the departure of the Barotse Paramount king to and from his summer and winter residences on and beside the Zambezi flood plain. The term actually means "Getting out of the water". As he is transported each way by longboat, there has to be sufficient water in the waterways to make the journey. And water is weather dependent: if there is enough rainfall between December and March, *Kuomboka* can happen, and the King can leave his summer residence in Lealui, to go and reside on higher ground on the flood plain margins at Limumunga. The journey also has to be undertaken at full moon time, when the omens are felt to be favourable.

The same is true for the return journey, for which there is a smaller, but no less dramatic ceremony. The King now sets sail with his wives and retinue, and is paddled back to his flood-plain residence at Lealui. Either way, the trip takes about six hours, which for the paddlers means six hours of intense, back-breaking physical effort.

Heather and I were fortunate enough to witness the latter ceremony. As it was not announced publicly, we responded to a rumour which Kevin and Karen Brandt, our missionary friends had heard, drove out with them over the flood plain, and waited.

It was soon clear that the King's (the *Litunga's*) return was imminent. Heightened police presence, though very unobtrusive; crowds gathering with mounting excitement; a sense of expectancy in the air.

The first glimpse was of a lurching elephant about a mile away across the plain. Not a real animal, but a massive effigy. We could make out peoples' heads below it, and realised soon that the elephant was on the roof of the cabin of the longboat. Drumming and shouts carried across the river and swamp-land to where we were waiting. The noise was increasing all the time, and over the next hour rose to a crescendo.

We had been standing under palm-trees, but Heather and Karen left us men to go to the other side, where apparently the wives' boat would dock. I have a treasured picture of Heather – a lone white figure in a sea of black ones – joining in the growing party spirit with appropriate quiet enthusiasm.

Before us was a broader stretch of quiet water, where they would all arrive. The first to turn the corner and come into closer view, were four canoeists, standing and propelling themselves expertly in a circle. These were the advance guard. And then, all of a sudden, the longboats were upon us. How impressive! What a din! The distinctive black and white stripes on the vessels' sides became a blurr, as the brown bodies of the rowers synchronised in perfect unison, to bring their *Litunga* to shore and home.

Each boat had perhaps one hundred oarsmen. There was smoke from on-board cooking fires, which mingled with the steam from over-heating bodies. And cool as you like, the King emerged from his on-board shelter, stepped out beneath his elephant, and on to the shore. We couldn't take it all in. All sorts of mini-ceremonies and gifts were being offered and accepted. It is the Lozi people, whose language is Silozi, who are the traditional rulers of the Barotseland kingdom. So many men wore Lozi dress, with red berets and tartan kilts, though strangely for us, the King himself wore a dark, very Western suit and tie! We learned later that he does also own, and often wears decorative ceremonial attire. We guessed this was probably just a very small *Kuomboka* for him.

But it was a privilege for us to be present, and it had been a marvellous day. The knowledge that this was not all for show, but an ancient tradition carried on through centuries, added authenticity to the occasion. I only saw one other white man - French I think - apart from ourselves.

And yet... even while the *Kuomboka* pageantry was at its boisterous height, we knew that far from the madding crowd, a comparatively small group of seventeen translators were working away quietly in five local languages. On the quiet hillside of Mutoya not so far away, a few more small steps were being taken towards the Word of God becoming available for the people of Western Province.

Back to my Roots

By the title I mean "Back to living in Belfast, where I was born."

I intended this final chapter to be full of wise reflection on life, the summation of all the experiences I have been privileged to enjoy. Well, there is bound to be some reflection, whether there is any wisdom the reader can judge.

Newcomers to Northern Ireland will not fail to notice that in the towns and cities, there is a church on practically every corner. In the rural areas, small mission halls abound too. We are truly spoilt for choice.

Church style

It has often struck me how a Christian's choice of church in which to worship may have more to do with psychological preference than the niceties of theology.

What follows is full of generalisations, so we must start with the proviso that Individuals can't be rigorously pigeon-holed, and there are other factors such as family background which come into play.

That said, to their meetings the **Quakers** tend to attract those of a quiet, contemplative disposition, who are comfortable with silence, and seek God in it. In their services they give God room to prompt them, rather than crowding Him out. They seek inner realities rather than outer symbolism, and so do not practise the sacraments and ordinances which other churches do. Historically, they did not want to take the oath of allegiance to enter university or college, so many clever Quakers turned to business and were highly successful: Barclays (banking); Cadbury's and Fry's (chocolate); Clarks (shoes); Huntley and Palmers (biscuits); Rowntree's (sweets); Nike, Sony and of course Quaker Oats - all became household names.

Apart from one meeting on a Sunday, and perhaps one during the week, they meet and visit in each other's houses for fellowship. Thus, they attract introverts, but also those with a strong social conscience who want to improve the lot of those around them. Bessbrook in N Ireland is a prime example. Not only did the Quaker employers provide jobs in this village, they catered for the whole person well ahead of their time, with housing surrounding expanses of grass on which children could play.

Heather's mother's family were Quakers.

My father's side was **Church of Ireland**. Traditionally, those who like to be private about their deep innermost feelings or their faith, and those who like tradition and repetition itself and feel comfortable with that, are attracted to Anglicanism. Why be spontaneous in worship, if you have centuries of hymns, liturgies and the toil of wordsmiths to benefit from? You follow in a long line of believers, and you like to genuflect with the best of them at the same point in the service every week. This appeals to personalities who relax in a structured setting, led by ministers who respect protocols and understand what comes next.

Heather's father's family was **Methodist**. She grew up feeling a duty of care to her wider family circle, to the church, to the community in which she lived. Church services were very inclusive, body life very evident. There was an egalitarian atmosphere between male and female, young and old, with relationships based on mutual respect rather than position held. This denomination seems to suit those who like consensual decision-making, and believe in service to all.

Philip's mother grew up **Presbyterian.** Apart from a tolerance of committees, to be a good Presbyterian you need to be endowed with a considerable dose of fairness and a sense of justice. And you have to like your minister, for you need to respect the one at the top, and the way they do things. Then you can be loyal in the way you want to be. You want the right things to be done in the right way.

To be a good **Baptist,** you need to be able to smile, and to hold your breath under water. It helps to be able to sit absolutely still and not fidget when listening to a forty-minute sermon.

The **Brethren** suits those who are not keen on any outright human leader, and know how to be joyful without smiling too much.

For the **Pentecostals** it is hard to sit still, or to be silent for long. This sounds like a place for the extroverts.

Charismatics and **New Church** people love spontaneity and the unpredictable; tradition and how things were always done is not so important to them. The present and the future are what matter.

So there we are. Which church suits your personality? You have quite a choice in our wee country, and we haven't even touched on dress code yet...

The lyrics of Church music

If ever there was a hot potato, church music is one.

We mentioned "hobgoblins" earlier. There is little place for them in most churches today. But after one has sung "I love You" to the Lord for the umpteenth time, one yearns for a wee hobgoblin to feed the mind as well as the emotions.

There are Christians who believe we shouldn't be singing any hymn or chorus composed after about 1980. They argue for relevance. As Bible translators we believe in translating into a language that is clear and natural, so we can go along with this view to a certain extent. However, does this mean that we only sing words that we use in our active vocabulary, or do we include the treasury of words often lying dormant in our passive vocabulary?

The average person's active English vocabulary is only around half of their passive vocabulary. According to lexicographer and dictionary expert Susie Dent, "the average active vocabulary of an adult English speaker is around 20,000 words, while his passive vocabulary is around 40,000 words." (Cited in article - *Is Your Vocabulary Higher Than the Average Adult?* In Direct Expose by **Lyn Kelly**, 23rd July, 2017.) English is reckoned to possess almost a million distinct words.

And God understands every one of them, plus all the millions of words that exist in the world's approximately 7000 languages. So why do we use such a limited number of them in our modern worship?

Four houses we have owned in Ireland

I promised earlier we would come back to visit houses Heather and I have lived in. So here goes with our quest for a first one.

51, Old Holywood Road, Belfast

"Philip, go and knock on their door, and tell them we'd like to live there!"

At least, this is my memory of what Heather said. Heather's

recollection is a little different, more like: "Philip, would you ever go and ask those folk would they care to move house?" At that point, in 1977, we had been married for almost a year. We were teaching languages in secondary schools, and the school year was drawing to a close, so both staff and students were looking forward to the summer break.

For our first year of marriage, we lived in one half of a gate-lodge. This quaint little lodge, with its older red-brick exterior, had been fully renovated inside by my uncle Bobby, who was a builder - like many Bobs. Its setting was in the leafy suburbs of East Belfast, close to the side gates of Stormont, the Parliament Buildings. From it we could take refreshing walks along the wide avenues of Belmont, in adjacent parks, or up into the Holywood hills towards Craigantlet, where C.S. Lewis loved to roam as a boy growing up.

And this is how Heather came to say what she said, while out on one of these walks. The house in question was a two-storey cottage, red-brick of about the same vintage as our rented gate-lodge. It was semi-detached to an identical one, and there was another pair of cottages – so there were four in all. They were very picturesque and chocolate box attractive, though in need of some tender loving care.

Imagine our surprise, then, when on our return from school summer holidays, we saw a "For Sale" sign outside two of them!

The short story is that we bought one, Heather's cousin Jennifer bought the other, Bob the builder totally renovated the inside, coughing through dust, and ancient lath and plaster, to bring it beautifully up to date. He did the same for Jennifer's cottage.

We bought it for nine thousand pounds, spent a further ten on improvements, received a grant for five, so ended up with a lovely wee dwelling for fourteen thousand pounds. These days they would call it a *bijou residence*.

We lived in it for a year while studying at the Irish Baptist college nearby, attending with baby Joy in a carry-cot. Soon, though, it was time to go abroad with Wycliffe Bible translators, so we let out the cottage for our time in Africa, up until 1990. The three renters we had while abroad all loved the wee house, and made us offers to buy it, but we weren't for selling at that point.

20, Belmont Park, Belfast

When we came back from Ivory Coast to spend our next stint in the Old Holywood Road house, our family had increased to five, with Rachel and Hilary being born in 1982 and 1987. We soon realised that for the three girls all to share the tiny second bedroom was too much of a challenge, so I went for late night walks in the neighbourhood to look for a suitable, bigger house.

Belmont Park was a mile or so closer to the centre of Belfast, but still in a quiet area. Shops, Post Office, home bakery and several good schools were all within walking distance. Some said that they moved house to this part of town, simply to be closer to the *Golden Crumb* bakery, with its superb cinnamon loaves and wheaten bread. For us, the main reason was that we could have four bedrooms, and space for a growing family. Financially, No 20 was originally a stretch for us to buy, but in retrospect, we are very grateful that this house appreciated in value so much over the fifteen years we owned it. We were able to borrow on it to help us through increasing costs in Africa, and to assist with the children's schooling at home in Ireland. We sold it in 2006, at the height of the housing market boom in N Ireland, and so were able to purchase Heather's parents' home in Waringstown, as her mother was downsizing to a bungalow now that Heather's father Cecil had died.

1, Tudor Lodge, Waringstown

Because it had been in the family, this large chalet bungalow was familiar to us, and to our children. It was now under new management, however, so there was no longer a sweetie cupboard overflowing with goodies for many grandchildren, and not a few immature adults!

In the planning of this house, Heather's mum and dad had deliberately included a long bedroom on the upper floor. It ran the width of the house, and the idea was that the two younger sons – Heather's two youngest brothers - could share this bedroom when they were home, and be far enough away from each other not to fight. This purpose-built room also afforded a space where we could stay as a missionary family on furlough, parents at one end, children at the other, with a dividing curtain to help everyone to sleep.

Heather enjoyed the many flowering shrubs in the garden of Tudor Lodge, and the gracious reception rooms, decorated with her mother's aesthetically pleasing touch, which Heather shares.

We enjoyed living here for eleven years, which takes us up to 2017.

Apartment 2, Bethshean Lodge, Finaghy

This is where I am writing from today.

Life takes surprising twists and turns. We did not imagine we would be back living in Belfast, and yet here we are. The idea of moving back came to us both, after a visit to my brother David and his wife Ruth, who live in the next door apartment.

In this respect it is ideal. We can look out for each other and when Heather and I are travelling abroad for translation consulting, the apartment is more secure. It is an easy care flat, with the outside lawn and hedge being tended by practical groundsmen.

To downsize so drastically has been the challenge. As missionaries, it is hard to throw out anything that could have been put to use in the countries where we work. But then, we have had some practice in small space living in the Castlerock studio. Our marriage having somehow survived that, who knows, if God wills, we may even get to celebrate a Golden anniversary in Bethshean Lodge.

Letter to Grandchildren

Dear Famous Five,

This book was dedicated to you at the beginning, so you should have the last word from me too!

When I asked your mothers what it was that I had said to them growing up that they would remember me for, they said:

"You regularly asked us, 'What does it matter what other people think?'" Implied was: "It doesn't matter what other people think!"

Now, it does matter a wee bit what others think, but what I meant was that our lives should not be controlled by that, for that is a kind of fear.

The motto at Vavoua International School, which Joy, Rachel and Hilary attended in Ivory Coast, was taken from Proverbs 9:10 (NIV): *"The fear of the Lord is the beginning of wisdom."* So it is wise to fear the *Lord*, rather than people. Not the kind of fear that means you are scared of Him, but that you listen to what He tells you, and try to obey Him above all else.

There was a grandad who once said this to his son, who then passed it on to his own child:

> "Take my words to heart.
> Follow my commands, and you will live.
> Get wisdom; develop good judgment.
> Don't forget my words or turn away from them.
> Don't turn your back on wisdom, for she will protect you.
> Love her, and she will guard you.
> Getting wisdom is the wisest thing you can do!
> And whatever else you do, develop good judgment.
> If you prize wisdom, she will make you great.
> Embrace her, and she will honour you."
> (Proverbs 4: 4-8 NLT)

My prayer for each one of you is that you will fear the Lord, and I know that He will give you the wisdom you need for living. Each generation has hard things to face, and yours will be no exception; but trust God and He will guide you through it, and give you discernment to choose the right path, for you.

Dance to God's music, listen out for the beat of His tamtam.

Postscript

This book would not be complete without my acknowledging the special contribution of certain friends. Firstly, my sister Pamela, whose phenomenal memory for detail helped me recall a lot from our early family life. Such a laugh we had! Then, many thanks must go to David McFarland, for his expertise in the final editing and production, and the fellowship we enjoyed during the process. Finally, I am indebted to the Edgehill and Waringstown Christian Writers' Groups for their encouragement and feedback, as they listened with such patience to many of the stories.

My perspective is that I am an ordinary guy, who has had the privilege to live in some exotic places because of my father's job, and also due to my own service among some neglected people-groups around the world. In the course of my work, I have met some extraordinary people, both members of these groups and those who try to help them by coming alongside.

What has most impressed me has been the humility I have observed in certain top linguists and top anthropologists, and the profound patience of hundreds of Bible translators in their quest to provide God's word for the world's peoples in their own languages.

If even a few of their admirable qualities rub off on me, simply through spending time with them, I will be more than happy.

Printed in Poland
by Amazon Fulfillment
Poland Sp. z o.o., Wrocław

53221432R00132